Forty Plus

Graham Wilson & Chris Harle

FORTY PLUS

Challenge walks in the north of England

illustrated by Chris Harle

High Tor Publications

First published in Great Britain in 2015 by
High Tor Publications
38 Hackney Road, Matlock
Derbyshire DE4 2PX

ISBN: 978-0-9932807-0-2

Typeset in Adobe Jenson Pro
Printed and bound in the United Kingdom
by T J International Ltd, Padstow, Cornwall PL28 8RW

Contents

How it all began   1

The nuts and bolts of the matter   4

THE WALKS

1 The Lang Stride   7
*A tramp around the gritstone edge that protects the outer
fringes of the northern uplands.*

2 Harrier's Delight   19
*A traditional yomp over the once forbidden and still rarely
visited Forest of Bowland.*

3 The Cumbrian Watershed   31
*A high-level traverse of the Lakeland Fells, taking in the
former county tops of Lancashire, Cumberland and
Westmoreland.*

4 A Bridge Far Enough   45
*An east-west peak and valley crossing of the Lakes that
traces, en route, the District's history and development.*

5 The Hot Trod   59
*This Northumbrian route picks its way carefully along
well-established tracks through otherwise inhospitable country.*

6 The Real Pennine Way?   71
*The nearest thing to a wilderness walk in England. Scarcely
a path in sight on these remote Durham moors.*

7 The Three Peaks and One or Two Others   83
*A roller-coaster of a route that follows the watershed of the
Yorkshire Dales.*

8 The M62 Roundabout   95
   Dodging the traffic to circle the interesting ground that lies
   between the satanic mills of south Lancashire and Yorkshire.

9 The Bakewell Pudding   107
   A delightful journey that connects the best of the White
   Peak. The going is easy, with no shortage of points of
   refreshment.

Baggers and Trotters
The story of long distance walking in the North of England   121

Postscript   130

Reader's Log   135

Note to Readers

Readers are reminded that although the information in this book is based on the authors' own experience, circumstances can change. This is particularly true of hilly countryside, through which the majority of these routes pass. It is the individual's responsibility to assess his or her ability to undertake the journey, or any part thereof, in the manner described.

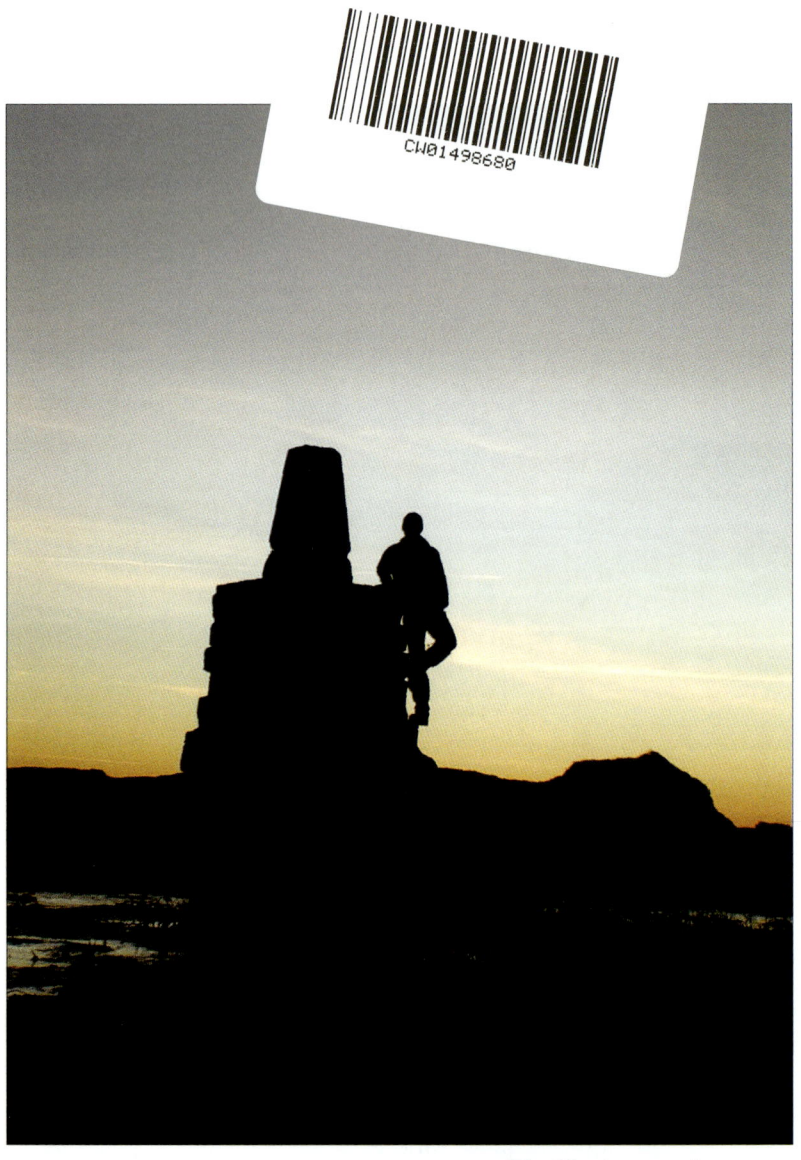

The Cheviot summit at sunset

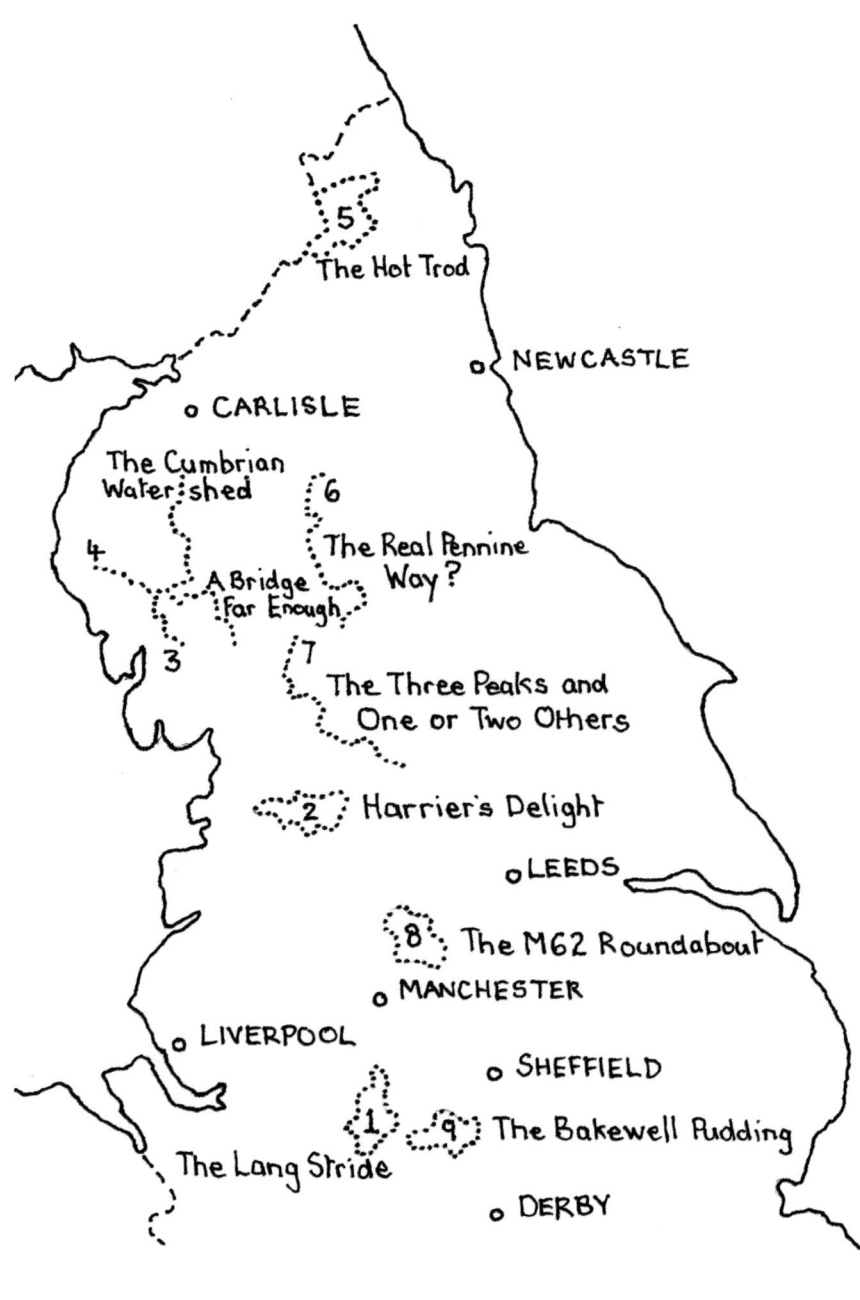

The Hot Trod

NEWCASTLE

o CARLISLE

The Cumbrian
Watershed

The Real Pennine
Way?

A Bridge
Far Enough

The Three Peaks and
One or Two Others

Harrier's Delight

o LEEDS

The M62 Roundabout

o MANCHESTER

o LIVERPOOL

o SHEFFIELD

The Bakewell Pudding

The Lang Stride

o DERBY

How it all began

It all started, appropriately enough, while walking through a cemetery. I was approaching my 40th birthday and could no longer convince myself that the natural fitness bestowed by youth and a once fairly vigorous lifestyle might still be called upon. The mirror doesn't lie and the choice was unfortunately simple—40 and fit or 40 and fat. In theory, the answer was obvious, but, as anyone who has passed the tipping point of innocence realises, theory and practice are rather different affairs. The momentary flash of inspiration, like most resolutions to improve my welfare, would probably have withered faster than the newly placed flowers I was passing, if it hadn't been for an idle comment made by a climbing acquaintance. 'Ever thought of trying the Bob Graham?'

The Bob Graham is a circular walk around the fells of Cumbria which starts and finishes in Keswick. I first became aware of it at a surprisingly early age when, to assist the annual family holiday, my father bought the appropriate copy of the famous Ward Lock Guides. Written by M J B Baddeley, *The Lake District* included a description of fell-walking as a competitive pastime, during which participants attempted to 'bag' as many summits in a day as they could. Like many others, the author had assumed that an unbeatable 'round' had been achieved in 1905, when A W Wakefield surpassed all existing records with a circuit that included twenty separately named peaks in a time of 22 hours, seven minutes.

Therefore, the attempts that followed concentrated on lowering the time rather than increasing the distance until, in the middle of the summer of 1932, Robert Graham, a guest-house proprietor in Keswick, hatched his grand design. Like Wakefield, he aimed to complete his round in less than 24 hours but, more ambitiously, to climb not twenty but 42 peaks, one for each year of his life. At 1.00am on June 13th he left Keswick and set off up the slopes of Skiddaw. Twenty-three hours and 39 minutes later he arrived back home, having covered not only Wakefield's summits but also a good number of outliers and a new set above Langdale.

It was a long way and such was the magnitude of the achievement that, when it came to judging how far Graham had walked, a certain amount of journalistic licence was employed and estimates approaching 100 miles were postulated. Nowadays, although the actual route over the intervening ground can vary, it is generally agreed that the distance is 65 miles plus the extra distance covered by ascending and descending 27,000 feet. Nevertheless, at somewhere around two and a half marathons and an ascent of Everest in a day, it was and is still a substantial effort and was justifiably reported at the time as a world record. It stood, as testimony to Graham's physical and psychological strength, for a remarkable 28 years. But times change and completion of the round is now a regular occurrence. Today the aim of serious fell-runners is to add more and more peaks within the allotted time.

I seem to remember that when Ron and I agreed our friend's suggestion was a good idea we were sitting comfortably in the bar of a public house. In the cold light of the next morning we began to take stock. The furthest I had ever run without stopping was about eight miles and the longest walk I had ever done was a round of the Lake District 3000ers, which was a good deal shorter and contained rather less up and down than the proposed venture. The only straw within reach was that the ascents of Skiddaw, Helvellyn and the Scafells had recently taken place, without too much trouble, whereas a much earlier attempt in my teens had ended in an ignominious lift from Seathwaite back to Keswick. Perhaps, I reasoned, when it came to fell-walking, I was now in my prime.

We decided on two things. First, we wanted to embrace the spirit of the founder and just set off one midsummer's day, rather than launch a military manoeuvre which would allow us to be 'paced' around the course by relays of support runners. Second, as part of getting fit for the effort we should, as well as inspecting the course, deliberately seek out hilly areas which were unknown to us. As well as novelty, the experiment produced some interesting moments—racing an oncoming train across a very narrow viaduct in Glen Orchy, dodging an avalanche on Helvellyn and crossing the Tees after a cloudburst, spring to mind—but the whole venture, from the Brecon Beacons to the far north of Scotland, opened

doors to parts of hilly Britain I had never really considered before and indirectly led to the existence of this book.

All the ground covered on the subsequent pages is in the North Country, which has more than its fair share of hills. According to one established estimate of England's 253 separate summits over 2000 feet, only two lie south of Sheffield. So, not surprisingly, it is home not only to England's highest mountain but also its highest inn (Tan Hill), village (Flash) and classified road (A689 at Killhope Cross). To find a route was merely a matter of picking an area and joining the dots. Such are the possibilities that, although we have inevitably 'trespassed' on such well-established thoroughfares as the Pennine Way and the Three Yorkshire Peaks, a good proportion of the descriptions that follow are well away from the beaten track.

All the routes are around 40 miles and although the experienced crow might estimate one or two of them a little under that distance, the actual course on the ground, taking into account ups and downs, circumnavigation of particularly boggy bits, etc, makes them all within the magic range of 40+. Each is designed to be done in a day and, assuming favourable weather conditions and long daylight hours, should be completed within twelve to fifteen hours. To allow ease of planning and the opportunity for reconnaissance, each route has been divided into four roughly equidistant sections and directions are included to the nearest available point of public transport. There are nine routes in all and if you desire the perfect ten, you can, of course, invent one yourself.

PS For those who have doubts about their capabilities or the worth of such a venture, I would draw attention to one Eustace Thomas, a dyspeptic and flat-footed Manchester businessman, who didn't begin serious walking until his forties. In his early fifties he became the first person to repeat Wakefield's round in a faster time and two years later became the first to ascend 30,000 feet in one journey. No doubt buoyed by these achievements, he put his foot on the accelerator and took up Alpine climbing to become the first Englishman to climb all the 83 peaks over 4000 metres. At the age of 90 he was still to be found wandering around the Arctic wastes.

The nuts and bolts of the matter

What follows is an explanation of how the book was put together. As joint authors, we agreed on a basic philosophy, i.e. it should be a combination of maps and words that would give an overview of each route, a feeling for what the reader is about to undertake and the nature and variety of the country that he or she will be passing over.

To that end, I took responsibility for the narrative and Chris for the maps, following an up-to-date checking of all aspects of the routes. The latter is particularly important for, though my descriptions are founded on experience, my knowledge and memory is stretched over a number of years. The general topography may well have stayed the same, but the furniture tends to move—a path closed here, a bridge built there. This is especially true if the Forestry Commission is involved as, like Macbeth's nemesis, it is prone to shifting the timber to confuse the onlooker.

We agreed an overall map should appear before the text for each route, so that readers could familiarise themselves with the task in hand, then we should follow the text with more detailed maps dividing the route into roughly equal-length sections. The scale of these maps is consistent throughout. It was hoped this combination would enable readers to get an overall sense of the undertaking and enable them to plan and, if necessary, reconnoitre the route beforehand. To assist that eventuality, possible escape routes have been indicated and particularly indefinite sections have been magnified in adjacent panels.

Instinctively, we felt North should be at the top of the page. Although this is possible with the routes running north/south and with circular routes where the longer axis lies predominantly in that direction, a problem arises when the direction of travel is for the most part along an east/west axis. As the book is in portrait format, it is impossible, in such cases, to keep North in its accustomed position without offending either or both the desired constraints mentioned above.

The solution adopted for this particular problem was to have West at the top but label the detail so that the words ran parallel to the spine rather than across the page in the orthodox manner. This would encourage the reader to rotate the guide to read the legend and therefore, when viewing the map, to 'look North' as before. This may appear to some unnecessarily complicated, but for those weaned on Wainwright's *Pennine Way Companion*, where the description of the route starts at the foot of the last page and works backwards and upwards to the beginning of the book, it should be simplicity itself.

As far as the narrative is concerned, it is heavily influenced by an article written by Menlove Edwards in the 1937 Climbers' Club *Journal*. He is reviewing the Fell & Rock's *Rock Climbing Guide to Scafell*. After praising the attention to detail, he gets down to cases and reaches the conclusion that the guide is fundamentally wrong. He likens the method of description to that of a spotlight highlighting the minutiae but throwing no light on the route as a whole, and points out that, as a result, you have no real idea where you are. If you get lost, the only option is to start again at the beginning, not an attractive proposition if you have already laboured for several hours. Although this was a rock climbing guide, we felt his observations applied equally to a walking version. Moreover, Edwards felt a guidebook should inform and entertain rather than merely instruct. Users should have the choice to select what was liked or found helpful and to disregard what was not. It is in that spirit our description is written.

All the above is based on the assumption that the reader accepts that the only true guidebook is the relevant OS map and possesses and is prepared to use the appropriate version, particularly when attempting any route that crosses remote and, at times, featureless terrain. And, aside from the question of safety, we would strongly recommend a previous glance at the relevant sheet, as one of the great pleasures in walks of this kind is the planning that goes on beforehand. There is little better than, on a winter's evening, to chuck another log on the fire, sweep the domestic debris from the kitchen table and, with a half-decent malt to hand, spread out the chosen portion of the Ordnance Survey like some multicoloured

tablecloth. The eye can see the land as it rises and falls, sweeping across an irregular mosaic of rock and water. As they smooth the creases, fingers transmit the vibrations of generations that have already walked the ground—to hunt, fight, farm, then finally trade—a palimpsest of human ingenuity eking out an existence from the shortest of commons. In easier times, we add our fresh footprint but, happily for us, the challenge is now of our making.

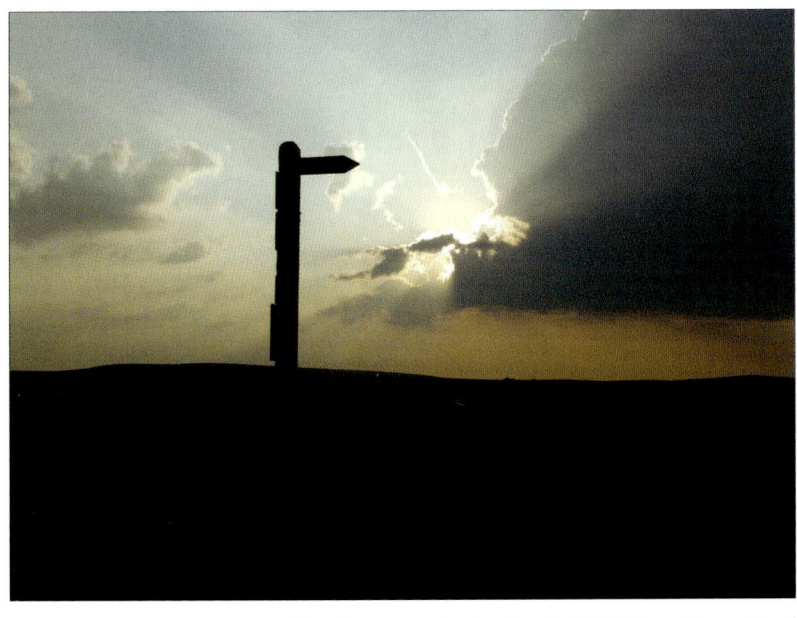

Looking towards the Cat & Fiddle from Dane Head

1 The Lang Stride

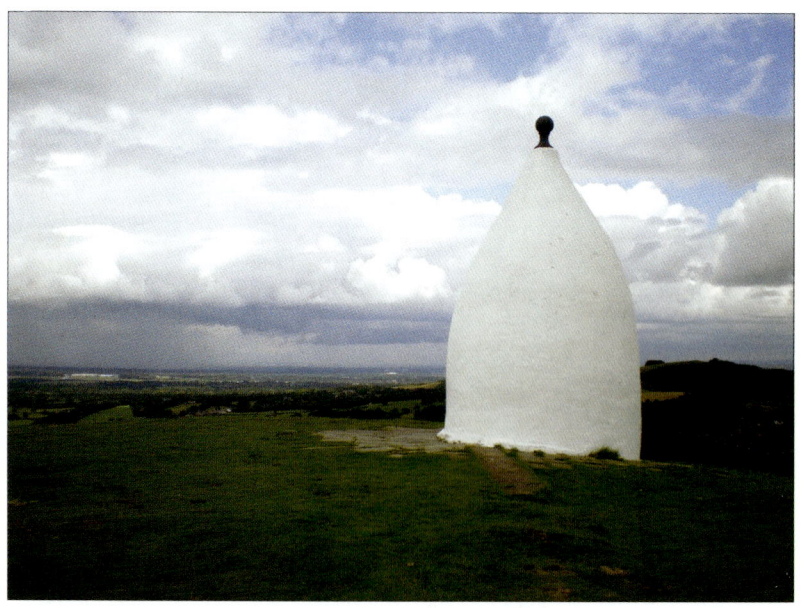

White Nancy on Kerridge End

1 The Lang Stride

Distance: 40.25 miles/64.4km
Ascent: 7050'/2150m
Start & finish:
Pym Chair car-park
(SJ 994 768)
Maps: OS Explorer
1:25,000: OL24
White Peak area
(the 2009 edition
covers most of
the route).
OL1 Dark Peak
covers the area
north of
Brink Farm.

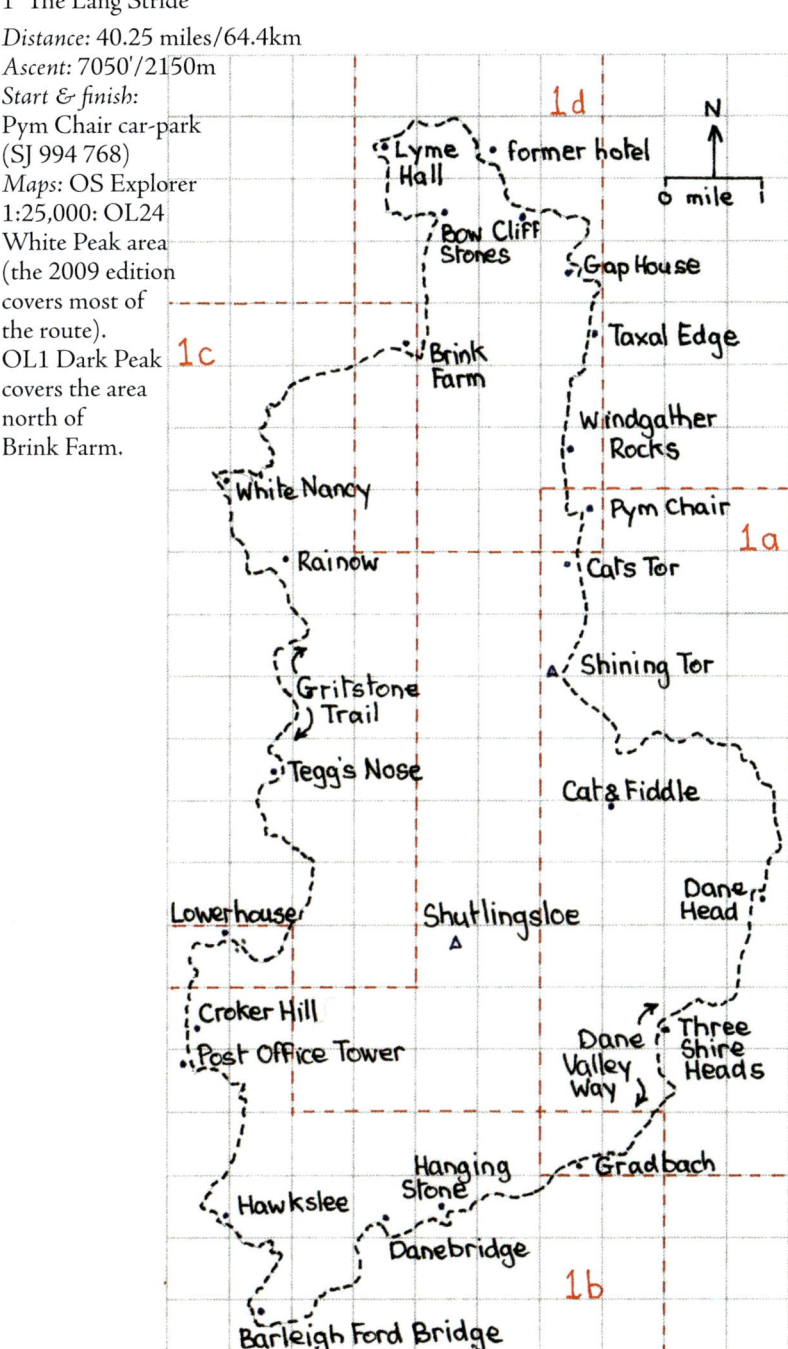

8

The land erupts out of Macclesfield in the east, travels a few miles, then falls with equal suddenness into Buxton on the west. But the ground that separates the two towns is no featureless plateau. Once you have left the car-park at Pym Chair and begun to climb the gently undulating ridge that leads to the highest point in Cheshire you realise that you are balancing on the rim of a bowl or, rather, a series of dips and hollows, each containing ancient tracks and lanes that ferret their way from isolated farms to nonconformist chapels and the occasional public house. This oval of land is the last redoubt of the northern highlands. To the south there is the odd bump or two that wrinkles the carpet of relative prosperity as it spreads to the south coast, but never again in England will you stand on such high ground until you reach those other Tors that sprout from the wastes of Dartmoor. This is the end of the North, and as the jaggers and their loaded pony-trains breasted the final ridge and looked down on the Cheshire Plain with its slower, broader streams, they must have breathed a sigh of relief.

The paved way to Shining Tor bears witness to the popularity of this section of the walk and not without reason, for the view from the Trig Point allows the memory of the map to become the image of your eye. The view is extensive, so it is worth pausing here to get your bearings. To the sou'sou'west stands Shutlingsloe, separate and somewhat aloof from the surrounding moors. This fine hill, the pivot around which The Lang Stride spins, is seen from all quarters of the route—sometimes shapely (here with more than a hint of the Matterhorn) but more often as a crouching, brooding hump. Further south lies the outline of the Roaches and the upper reaches of the Dane Valley, to the west, the Post Office Tower pinned on Croker Hill and, to the north, the rough bounds of Lyme Park. Much of your actual route is visible, a clockwise sweep that attempts to hold the high ground, only dipping from view to allow the first gatherings of the rivers Goyt, Bollin and Dane to escape towards the Atlantic Ocean.

But your way first is east, a helter-skelter that passes over the head of the Goyt before curving around to cross the Macclesfield/Buxton road, the delight of motorcyclists and reputedly the most

dangerous stretch of tarmac in England. Then south onto Axe Edge Moor to join the Dane Valley Way which eventually rolls its way downhill to the hamlet of Gradbach and beyond. This is the roughest and most remote part of the walk and is literally a minefield. Beneath our feet are scores of disused coal pits and even an underground canal that, at the behest of the Duke of Devonshire, produced and transported the low grade coal to fire the lime so essential to sustain the Industrial Revolution. The evidence of such man-made disruption has now disappeared and if it weren't for the whine of the Yamahas, you could imagine that little had changed over the ages.

In fact, closer inspection would reveal quite a flurry of relatively recent activity. First, still visible, the Cat and Fiddle, built to service the new turnpike, remains perched on the skyline above you. Burbage Edge holds under its tunnelled surface the remnants of the Cromford and High Peak light railway and below you the flooding of the Goyt Valley conceals the now submerged Errwood Hall. And even as the rough edges of human intrusion have been softened by time, so have those of the local inhabitants. At the end of this section lies Three Shire Heads, once the meeting point of the counties of Cheshire, Derbyshire and Staffordshire and renowned as a rendezvous for the criminal classes where robberies could be planned and 'flash' money change hands. Its dubious popularity was due to the ease with which the villains could step from county to county to avoid arrest by whichever parochial police force chanced to arrive. Now it is an innocent picnic spot and the setting of a hundred country calendars.

Next, we follow the river through fields where its tumble from Danebower gradually slows and spreads into the hamlet of Gradbach. As you approach there is a sense of a burgeoning community scattered around what was obviously a mill. Built by Thomas Dekeyne originally to spin flax, it meandered through the various textile options until finally settling for the manufacture of carpets. The mill wheel has gone but there is enough left of the casing to suggest it was designed for production on a fairly large scale. A scattering of cottages would once have housed local millhands, but now workers' cottages are country retreats and the

mill is a Youth Hostel. As with much of the United Kingdom, the transformation from manufacturing nation to service industry is complete.

Once Gradbach is left, the Dane Valley Way settles for a steady stroll along the riverbank past Wincle, then towards the A523 at Hugbridge. Your route, however, is made of sterner stuff. It climbs sharply to the Hanging Stone. If you follow the order of walks as they appear in the book, you are now as far east as you'll be for some time. Below you, the Dane makes its way to join the Mersey but just over the ridge above you lies Tittesworth Reservoir, the head waters of the River Churnet, which will eventually join the Trent and empty itself into the North Sea. But from this point on, all streams will flow west until you reach the eastern flanks of the Cheviot.

You have now entered a wooded world of myths, pagan beliefs and religious controversy. You might even meet a baby kangaroo. Part way up, look for a signpost, one finger of which points to Lud's Church. This, though walled in stone, is not a normal place of worship. A landslip has caused a deep narrow cleft to be riven in the hillside and has left a secret chamber, partially paved with worn stones and draped in moss and vegetation. Possibly, it was a place of pagan worship paying homage to the shaft of sun that fully pierces the gloom only at the summer solstice. More certainly, it was the inspiration for the Green Chapel that is central to the medieval poem 'Sir Gawain and the Green Knight' and in its course through history it has hosted the secret meetings of a variety of dissidents and dissenters. Even with the signpost, it is a difficult place to find, but it's more than worthwhile to take a breather and make the short diversion.

The baby kangaroo would, in fact, be a red-necked wallaby. In 1938 Courtney Brocklehurst, a member of the silk manufacturing family who lived at nearby Swythamley Hall, 'liberated' his private zoo onto the Staffordshire moorland. Among the contents were a flock of wallabies and an assortment of yaks, whose occasional appearance caused mixed reactions from both farmer and tourist. Most of the animals succumbed to the local weather but the wallabies, despite morbid announcements of their demise, have

been sighted on the estate as recently as 2009 and, as such, have outlasted the late departed owners. Not that you would accuse the Brocklehursts of being stay-at-homes. What with Courtney's safaris in the Sudan, Sir Philip supporting Shackleton on his polar expedition (hence the inn sign of an ice-fast 'Nimrod' on The Ship at landlocked Wincle), and his aunt, Marianne, organising a 1000-mile expedition down the Nile, admiring alike the local artefacts and physique of the steersman, you could say it was in the nature of the family to get about a bit.

After the Hanging Stone, the route drops down to Danebridge to rejoin the Dane Valley Way. But do not be deceived by the air of tranquillity. It was not that long ago that this stretch of the river was the scene for the most dubious of practices. A pedlar from Flash was making his way home when he stopped at a wayside inn. He was enjoying a pint when a child sidled up to him and started to pinch his arm and leg, remarking on the plumpness of the traveller and how his fingers would make 'good pies'. Understandably perturbed, the pedlar drank up and left, soon to be followed by the shouting of men and the baying of hounds. He escaped by fording the Dane to throw the dogs off the scent and hiding under the arch of a bridge until the hunt died down. The authorities were alerted and a raid on what are now the ruins of a home (which you may very well be passing) revealed evidence of murder and cannibalism on an industrial scale.

By this time, I imagine you will have had your fill of living in mortal fear of counterfeiters, cannibals, kangas and, for all I know, flying carpets and will gratefully accept the reassuring hand of Cheshire County Council as it offers you an escape route along its Gritstone Trail. You leave the Dane at Barleigh Ford Bridge and follow the signs to the trail's conclusion at Lyme Park. As a result of this bureaucratic solicitude, the next section of our route is well waymarked and should cause few navigational difficulties, least of all along the series of ridges that form the final step before the Northern wastes topple onto the Cheshire Plain. Looking up from that lower level, the skyline appears as an unbroken ridge walk, but closer inspection reveals hidden folds in the ground that shelter the villages of Sutton, Langley and Rainow from the worst

of the weather and you are forced to snake around these, holding the highest and best ground wherever possible. Nevertheless, if, as you walked along this section, you took a series of photographs from such strategic points as Croker Hill, Teggs Nose and Kerridge End, you could compose a complete panorama of the surrounding countryside, neatly framed by the Welsh hills to the west and the western Pennines to the north.

Once you have reached White Nancy, an eggish-shaped monument thought to have been erected to celebrate the Battle of Waterloo, the Trail swings towards the east and by the time you have reached Sponds Hill the view has changed. To the north lies the Dark Peak, dominated by the bulk of Kinder Scout, and, moving further round the compass, you see the valley that holds Todd Brook, cradled in the arm of the ridge that runs up to Shining Tor. But that is for later. Your way is still north, with a few sharp corners to negotiate before you can begin the home run.

At the Bow Stones (if you are feeling over-confident about your abilities, read the inscription on the gravestone) you climb a ladder stile, then plunge, leaving the rough pasture, into the parkland of Lyme Hall. This is the most delightful part of the walk, through tree-lined avenues, under the shadow of the Hall itself and across the deer park with its pools and pathways. The land is now the property of the National Trust but once was the home of the Legh family, whose unbroken line stretched back to Agincourt. It is renowned for its herds of red and roe deer which, as a traditional feature of Midsummer's Eve, were driven *en masse* through the Stag Pond towards the main buildings. It was obviously an impressive sight where, according to one witness, the antlers silhouetted against the light appeared as a wood marching across the waters.

The star attraction, however, was Joseph Watson, born in 1648 and at an early age appointed Keeper of the Parks. He was a master of his craft, once winning a 500-guinea bet for his employer by driving twelve brace of stags from Lyme to Windsor Park. He also lived life to the full. In 1725, Sir Peter suggested to Joseph's son that he should prepare to take over the job as it was only a matter of time before the 'old misfortune Friends and Drink' saw

his father off. By 1750, Sir Peter was long dead and Joseph was still capable of a six-hour stint with the local hunt. A prodigious feat—though probably not for a man who, before he died in 1753, had seen the back of six Monarchs, a Protectorate and 70 years of marriage.

Once the parkland is passed, the route skirts what was once the Moorside Hotel (an over-ambitious location, given its height and approach by a minor, often snowbound road) before you descend the final downhill slope to cross Todd Brook at Kishfield Bridge. You are now, at last, at the base of the ridge leading to Shining Tor. Rights of Way cross fields and after negotiating the B5470 at Gap House you are once more on Access Land. The ridge, conveniently, starts to flatten out and offers a gentle uphill stroll along Taxal Edge and past the climbers on Windgather Rocks, the least intimidating of the Derbyshire gritstone edges, before once more reaching Pym Chair and the retrieval of the can of whatever satisfies carefully hidden beneath the car seat.

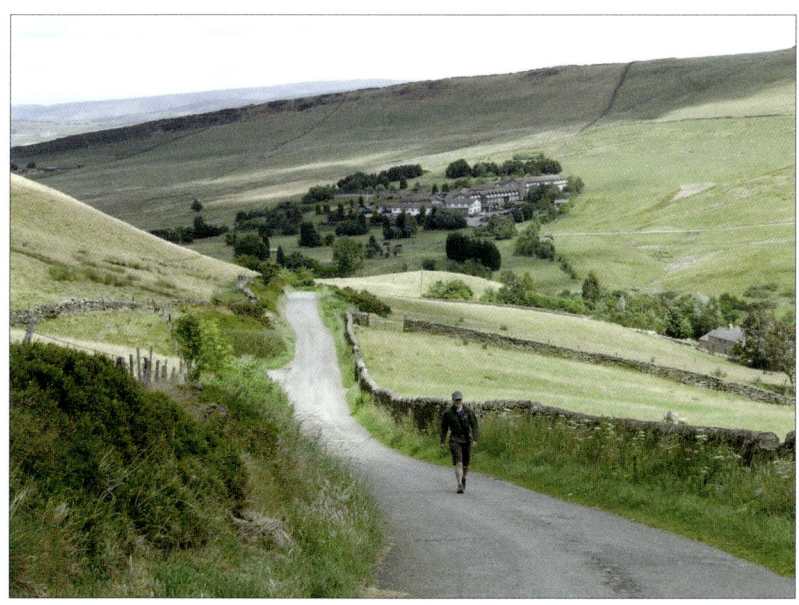

Near the Bow Stones, with former hotel in background (photo by Jane Harle)

The Lang Stride Map 1a

Start: Pym Chair car-park
(SJ 994 768)
Finish: Car-park on minor
road 500m east of
Gradbach Youth Hostel
(GR 998 662)
Distance: 10.75 miles/17.2km
Ascent: 1600'/488m

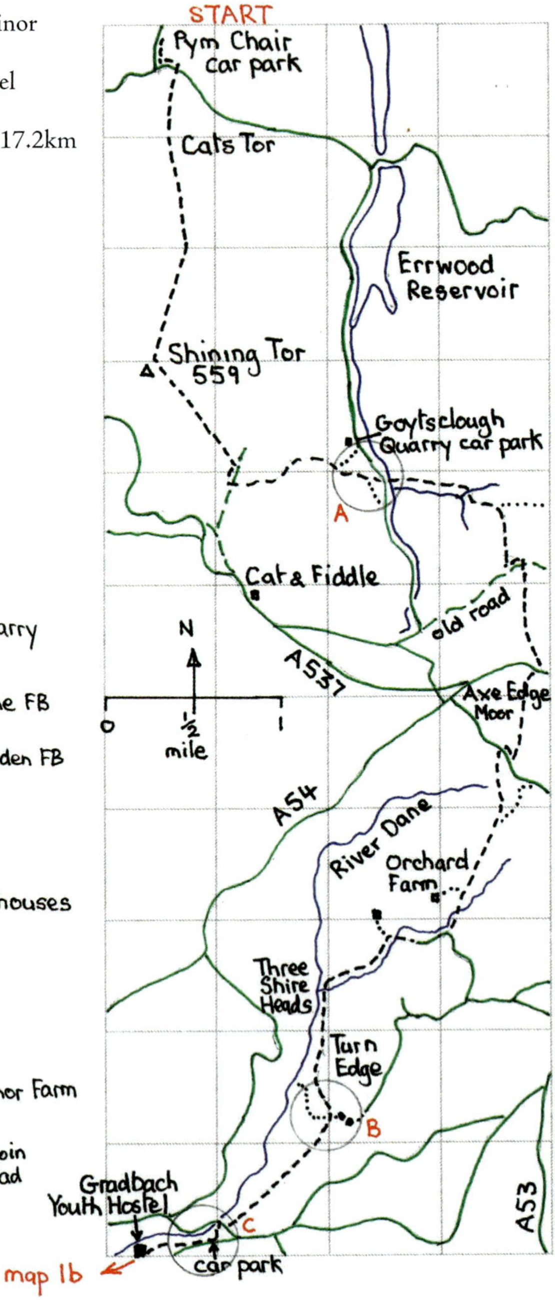

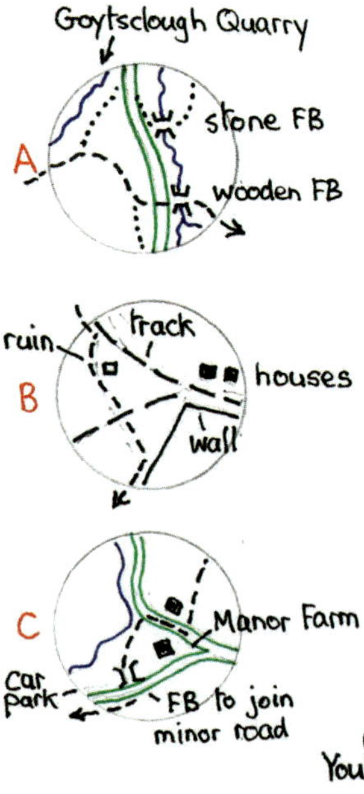

15

The Lang Stride Map 1b

Start: Car-park on minor road 500m E of
Gradbach Youth Hostel (SJ 998 662)
Finish: Lowerhouse (SJ 938 697)
Distance: 10.25 miles/16.4km
Ascent: 1750'/534m

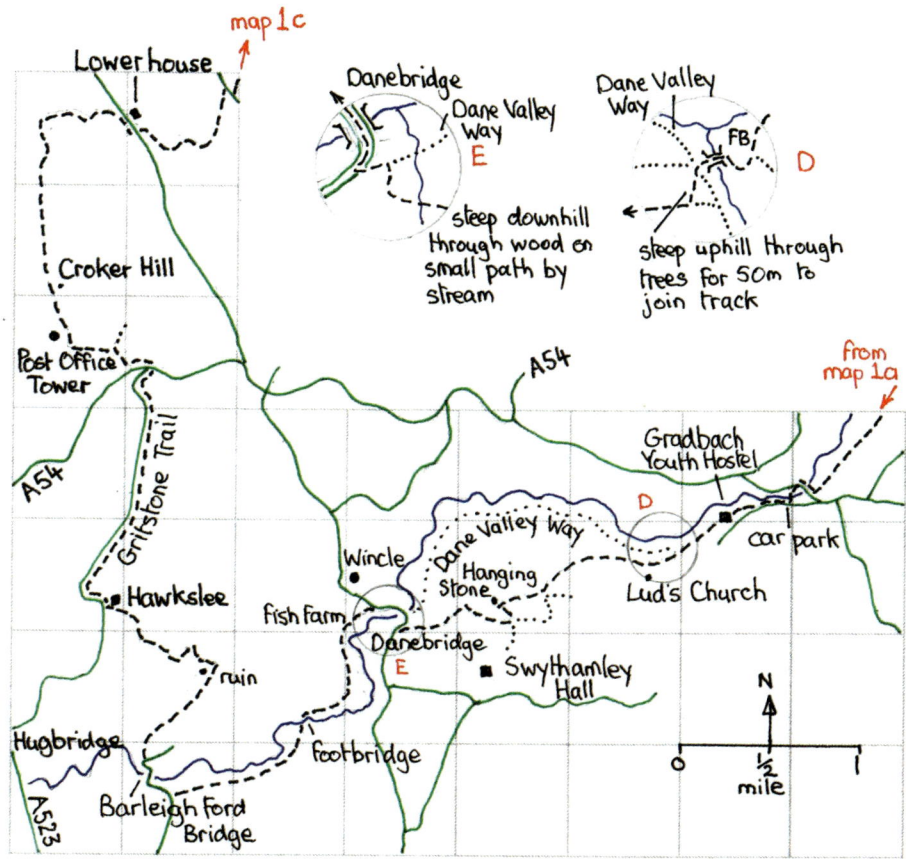

16

The Lang Stride Map 1c
Start: Lowerhouse (SJ 938 697)
Finish: Brink Farm (SJ 967 792)
Distance: 10 miles/16km
Ascent: 2400'/732m
This section continues to follow the Gritstone Trail throughout.

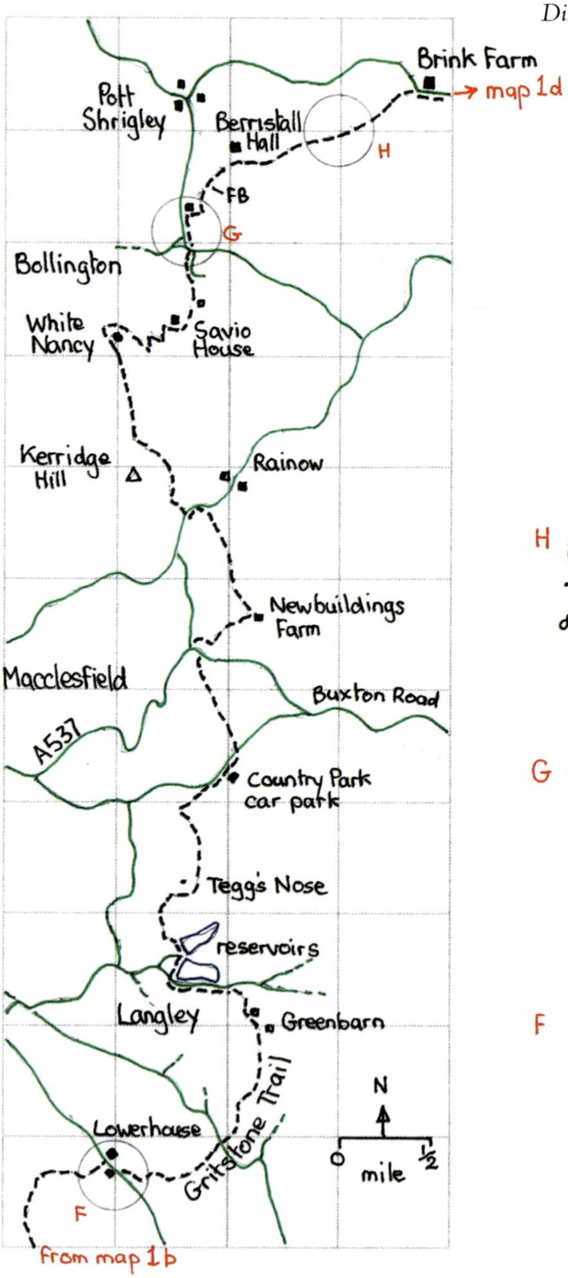

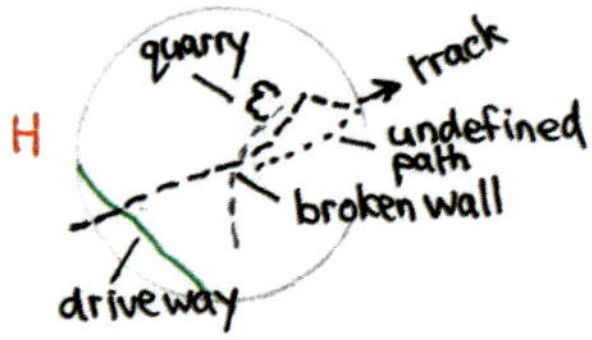

Brink Farm
→ map 1d

Pott Shrigley
Berristall Hall
H
FB
G
Bollington
White Nancy
Savio House
Kerridge Hill
Rainow
Newbuildings Farm
Macclesfield
A537
Buxton Road
Country Park car park
Tegg's Nose
reservoirs
Langley
Greenbarn
Lowerhouse
Gritstone Trail
N
0   mile   ½
F
from map 1b

H
quarry
track
undefined path
broken wall
driveway

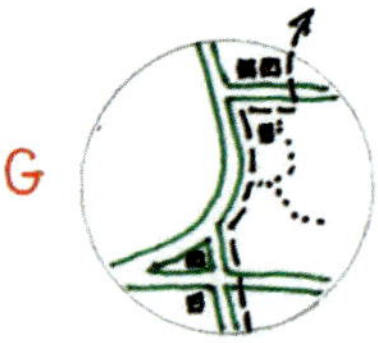

G

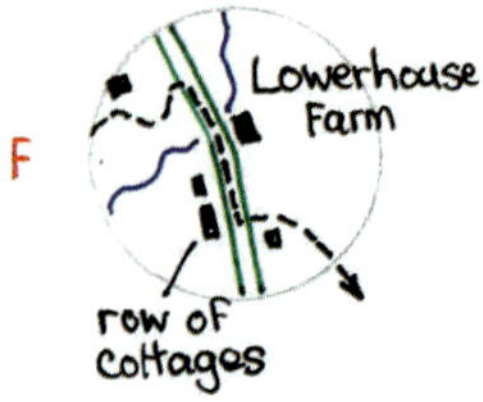

F
Lowerhouse Farm
row of cottages

17

The Lang Stride Map 1d
Start: Brink Farm (SJ 967 793)
Finish: Pym Chair car-park
(SJ 994 768)
Distance: 9.25 miles/14.8km
Ascent: 1550'/473m

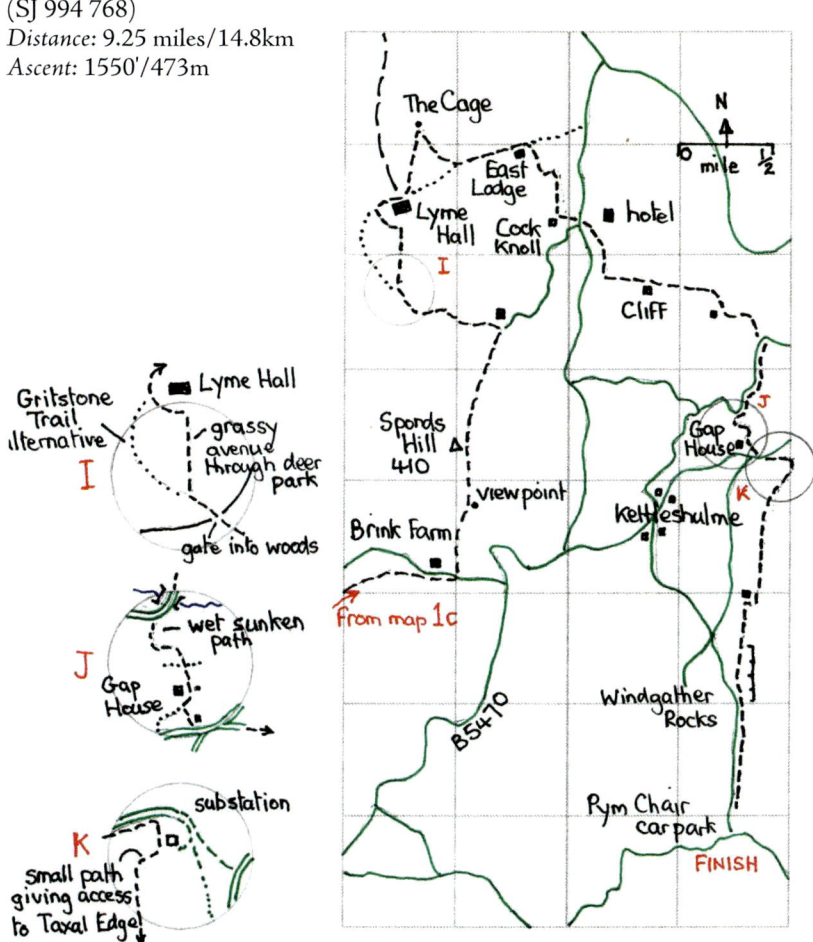

The Lang Stride Summary

A tramp around the gritstone edge that protects the outer fringes of the northern uplands. This circular walk has multiple escape routes and bus links to Buxton, Macclesfield and Whaley Bridge. The route passes close to a few pubs but no shops.

High point: Shining Tor 1834'/559m
Low point: Barleigh Ford Bridge 492'/150m

2 Harrier's Delight

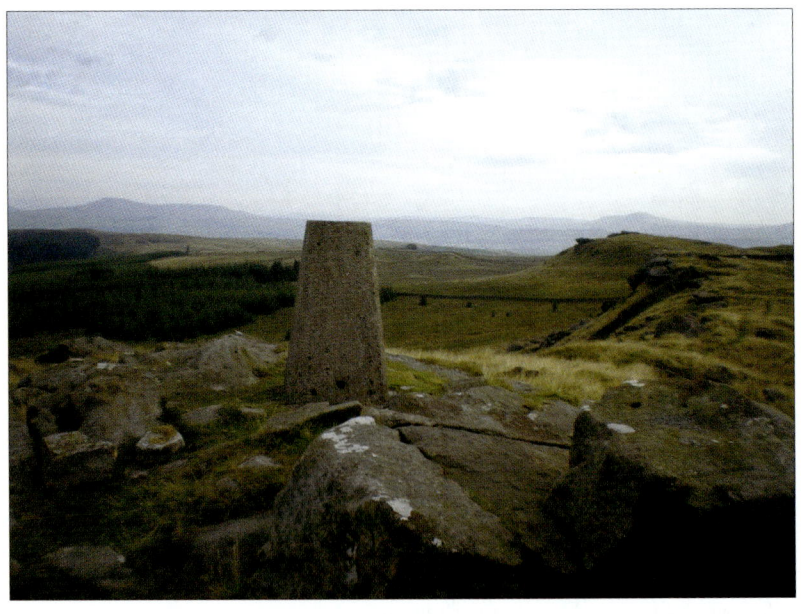

Ingleborough and Pen-y-ghent from Whelp Stone Crag

2 Harrier's Delight

Distance: 40.5 miles/64.8km
Ascent: 6000'/1830m
Start & finish: Slaidburn car-park (SD 713 524)
Map: OS Explorer 1:25,000: OL41 Forest of Bowland & Ribblesdale

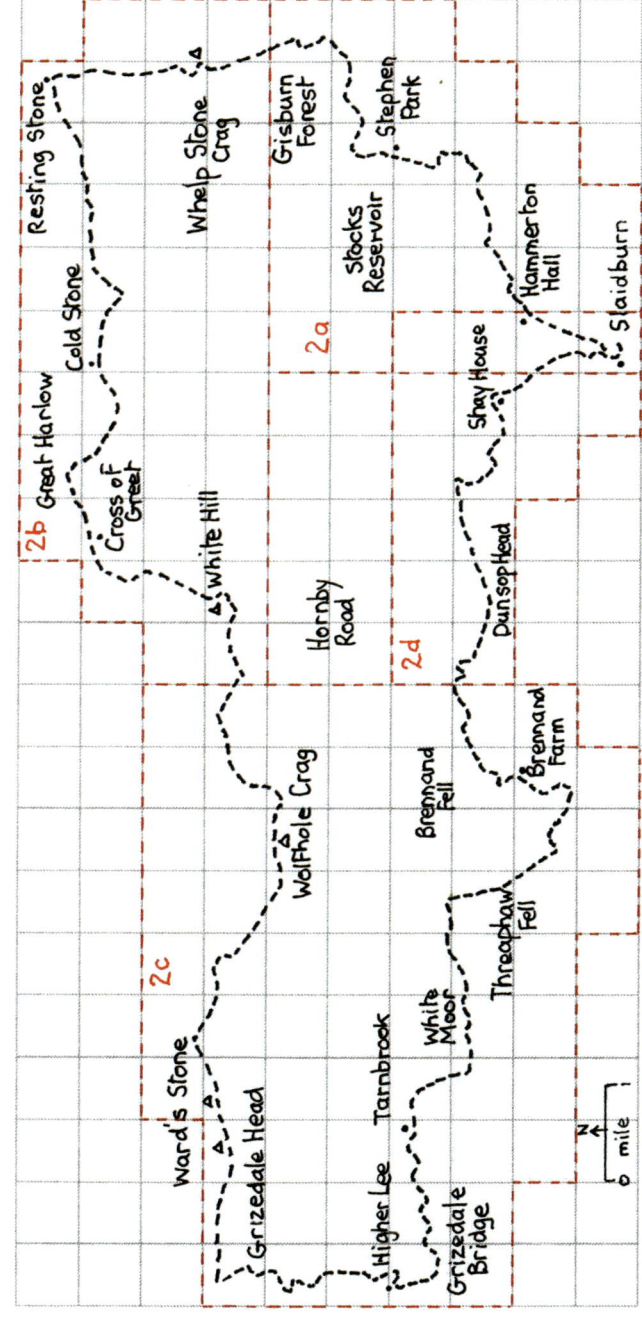

At the point in my life when I was force-fed the Children's Classics as opposed to my natural taste for the relative anarchy of *The Wizard* and *Hotspur*, I had thrust upon me Thomas Hughes' *Tom Brown's Schooldays*. A passage that sticks in my mind, or at least the one I best recall, is the description of The Great School Paper Chase, where our young hero, together with his friends East and Tadpole (so called because of the disproportionate size of his head) decided the time had come for them to take part in this annual athletic extravaganza. Misplaced enthusiasm, tinged with a touch of bravado, leads them to stick with the heroic Head of School rather than adopt the easier option of following the rest of the pack. The result of this detour is a struggle up hill and down dale through knee-deep Warwickshire clay. The cardinal sin of being late for 'Call Over' was the inevitable consequence of our harriers' decision, with the double blow of missing tea and a confrontation with the Head in his study. All, of course, ends well. They cadge a lift on the Oxford Stage (aka the Pig and Whistle) and the good Dr Arnold lives up to his firm, yet kindly, reputation.

As it turned out, wading through the cheerful sentimentality of *TBS* was an admirable preparation for similar trudges to come, particularly around the Forest of Bowland which can be considerably more cloying than Warwickshire clay. And if, in these straitened times, you think some form of 'pig' or 'whistle' will come to your rescue, you are mistaken. A bus occasionally brushes the area at Slaidburn in the south, or Wray in the north, but it will be of little use as, by then, you will have either abandoned the route half-way round or finished for the day. Although, as some sort of compensation, the walk tries to keep to established tracks, you have to be prepared for going that is at best 'soft to heavy'.

This sort of terrain in itself is not a bad thing. The blanket bog, that clings, supports a biodiversity of flora and fauna that, if left alone, prevents flash floods and ensures a good supply of drinkable water. It is also an important cog in a complex waste-disposal unit. Its very nature converts carbon dioxide into oxygen and to destroy it would have similar consequences to chopping lumps out of the Amazonian forest. Of course, a certain type of landowner has

done its best, destroying the fragile vegetation by allowing sheep to graze or setting it on fire to encourage new growth of grouse fodder. Nor are walkers free from blame, as continually following in the footsteps of others is the quickest way to long-term erosion. All concerned should consider putting the general good before their recreational interests and, if necessary, leave selected sections alone to allow opportunity for recovery.

The walk starts at the war memorial in Slaidburn, where you cross the bridge over Croasdale Brook and immediately pick up a footpath that leads along the bank of the River Hodder to Hammerton Hall. The presence of this building is a reminder of the long established and often turbulent history that lies behind the land you are crossing. Originally, it was a farm owned by the Hammerton family but matters changed when Sir Stephen chose the wrong side in the Pilgrimage of Grace. Henry VIII was not amused. Confiscation followed and the Greenacres who, we can presume, joined the right side, were given ownership. These nascent real estate entrepreneurs swiftly turned a penny by selling it to the Brere Family who built the hall you see before you. At which point, apart from the trifle of the valley being deliberately flooded, matters more or less settled down.

Where the path splits, you take the right fork past a barn and continue pleasantly via glimpses of Stocks Reservoir and Black House to a car-park on the edge of Gisburn Forest. This is all very easy going and, as it is not in any way typical of what is to come, it would be advisable to get the distance under your belt as quickly as possible. Cross the road and follow the obvious gravel track past Stephen Park to Heath Farm. The route taken is rather cir-cuitous but is preferable to the more direct overgrown forest rides or the shown rights of way. I may add that this will not be the last time in this series of walks when, on entering working forests, you may fail to find on the ground what you see on the map.

Once Heath Farm has been reached, you emerge from the trees and continue along the edge of the plantation until you can climb to the trig point at Whelp Stone Crag, where a magnificent panorama of the Yorkshire Peaks and Dales appears before you. The going now starts to get tougher but you soon reach the Resting Stone, a

rectangular lump of rock near the north corner of the forest. As it is too high to use as a seat or bench, the simplest explanation for the name is that the item being rested would have been a coffin. It was once a regular practice to carry the dead significant distances to ensure burial in consecrated ground, an act that involved considerable labour (on the link that joins Kirkby Lonsdale to Morecambe Bay there still remains part of a pulley system to lift the load over an awkward rocky section), but in this case matters are not so clear-cut as the stone is not *en route* to any obvious place of entombment. Whatever the reason, it is a convenient place to pause—not so much to catch your breath, you understand, as to take stock of the situation. You have now reached a boundary wall which you follow over Rock Cat Knott and Knotteranum to the minor road that crosses the ridge at Bowland Knotts. The ground continues to fall away sharply on either side, forming a fine ridge which continues over Cold Stone and Great Harlow to reach a second road at the remains of the Cross of Greet. Given the general reputation of the terrain of the Forest of Bowland, the going so far has been relatively easy but before you get too disappointed the stretch between the Cross of Greet and the Hornby Road starts to live up to expectations. Keep to the boundary as well as you can and cross White Hill to reach the gathering grounds of the rivers Roeburn and Whitendale. If drier land is sought, you can amuse yourself by climbing, before you reach the summit, a stone tower, an apparently functionless edifice but one which, with its three supporters to north and south, once formed a crucial part in the survey of the pipeline from Haweswater to Manchester.

The Hornby Road is a well-established and important link between the larger pockets of population to the south and the River Lune with its outlet to the sea. It was also a key section for those journeying north. If you know where and, more importantly, how to look, there are signs of the Roman road that was the main artery for transportation of provisions and reinforcements from the military garrison at Ribchester to the armies safeguarding Hadrian's Wall. Following the example of these early Italian engineers, local expertise constructed a pack-horse way that, once the watershed had been reached, held the contours in a high-level traverse just

below the skyline. Along it, place names like High, Middle and Lower Salter suggest the passage of sea salt transported from Morecambe Bay to the distribution centre of Whalley Abbey. Nowadays the road acts, for the most part, as a playground for those who choose to ride, run or walk in pleasant surroundings.

As well as today's followers of Tom Brown and his cronies, there are other harriers that enjoy the delights of this wet and wild wasteland. The ground we're crossing is part of the Abbeystead estate owned by the Duke of Westminster. Over the centuries a battle has been fought between the estate and the predators that threatened its game birds. Unfortunately for the hen harrier, its natural territory was the very moorland that best suited the rearing of grouse and of all the moorland of England, it chose the peat and heather of Bowland as its prime habitat. As God is on the side of the big battalions, the number of harriers dwindled almost to extinction and it required an Act of Parliament to make it illegal to kill the birds. Nevertheless the numbers remained fragile and there was much consternation of late when those at Bowland failed to breed.

Naturally, conspiracy theories abound. The birdwatchers claim that, despite the legislation, the gamekeepers are shooting or poisoning the birds. The Estate responds by suggesting it's all down to Open Access, with the walkers disturbing the nests. The pragmatists shrug their shoulders and point out there's bound to be a few casualties while creating a successful multi-million pound industry. There may, however, be another reason. A colony of herring gulls has recently been seen flocking beneath Wolfhole Crag in such numbers that, if you shut your eyes, you'd think you were in a fishing port when the fleet comes in. What these birds are doing there is anyone's guess. There is no obvious food source unless they've discovered the caches of grouse feed, or perhaps started to snaffle grouse eggs and newly born chicks. Maybe, as can happen, it is they who are scaring the harriers into infertility.

Whatever the truth, I fear the harriers will carry the can, as long as the sport of grown men remains on a par with small boys with catapults delighting in the sound of smashed glass. You could spend some time making up your own mind as you climb to

Wolfhole Crag but, if rewarded with a clear day, you will soon be turning your thoughts to the scene around you. As with Whelp Stone Crag, there are fine views of the Yorkshire Peaks but now, as you follow the ridge over Ward's Stone to the track at Grizedale Head, you can look south towards Pendle Hill and down the sun-lit slopes sweeping the foreground to the Trough of Bowland and, as you descend the track, catch glimpses of the very minor road that tenuously connects Slaidburn with the A6.

Once down at Higher Lee you take the road to Grizedale Bridge, then to the dead end at Tarnbrook. Although road walking is generally to be avoided, I would make an exception of the latter stretch of tarmac. The narrow, wooded lane running parallel to a stream gives a flavour of the whole of this secluded area. It has that air of timelessness that Edward Thomas captured so vividly in his poem 'Adlestrop'. People clearly live here, but any sign of habitation is discreetly hidden up winding drives and in the folds of the land. It must be a nice place to while away your time and so offers some compensation to those labouring under the burden of excessive wealth.

You now have to pay the price for dropping into the valley and there will be the odd rise and fall before you once more reach the Hornby Road. The first objective is any suitable point on the ridge running down from Brennand Fell to Threaphaw Fell. This is followed to Brennand Tarn, where you may see swans at the right time of the year, down to Brennand River, then along a track to Brennand Farm. Another rise and you are free of Brennands, before a fall brings you to Whitendale and deep into grouse-shooting territory. Leave the farm and climb for the final time to your last elevated viewpoint on Dunsop Head.

By this time you will have a good feel of the place and may consider you have, in some way, discovered the heart of the matter. And you would not be wrong, for a little to the north and west lies a stake, driven into the ground. This marks the exact centre of Britain. If you want to check it out for yourself, cut out a two-dimensional scale model of the landmass of the British Isles (all of them), then attempt to balance the result on the point of an HH pencil. Where it so does is the centre of Britain and with the aid of

a few complicated long-division sums you should be able to ascertain the exact point on the OS map you are currently holding in your hand. On the other hand, you could just trust Wikipedia.

Once you have reached the Hornby Road, make your way into and follow the pleasant meander of Croasdale back to your beginnings at the war memorial. As you once more reach Slateburne, to give the village its Domesday Book title, you might catch the strains of musical instruments. Probably not 'Hail the Conquering Hero Comes' but possibly another tune that lurks in the back of your memory. Slaidburn is a well-known piece for brass and silver bands and was composed by William Rimmer, winner of various Brass Bands Grand Challenge Cups, who, after a severe illness, retired to the area to convalesce. He so much appreciated the hospitality of the village, he wrote a piece in its honour, then stayed there for the rest of his life. But it may be by now you would prefer to march to a different tune. If so, hasten to the Hark to Bounty and, provided you can add your cheery 'Adsum' before the 'call over' imposed by the licensing laws, judge the hospitality for yourself.

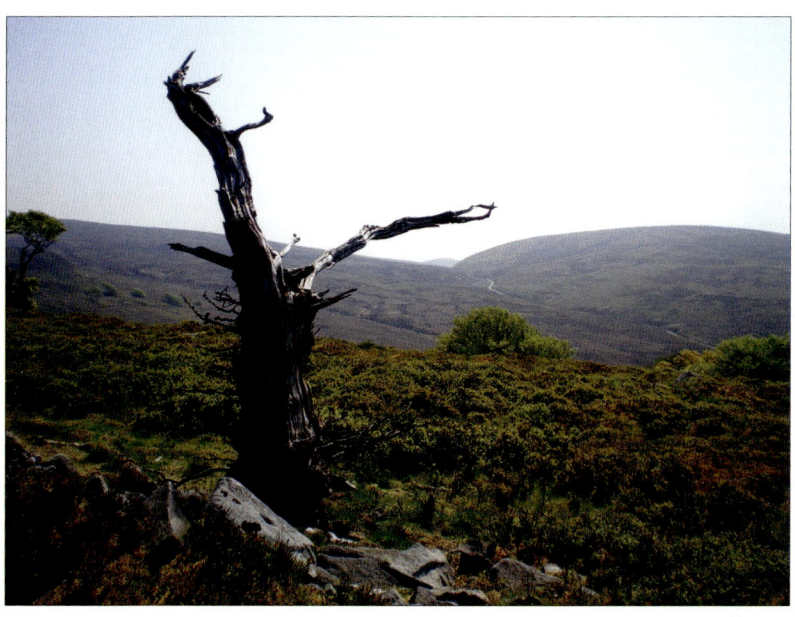

The Trough of Bowland from White Moor

Harrier's Delight Map 2a

Start: Slaidburn car-park (SD 713 524)
Finish: Gisburn Forest just N of Heath
Farm (SD 761 580)
Distance: 6.25 miles/10km
Ascent: 920'/280m
An easy start, gently ascending on good
paths and forestry tracks.

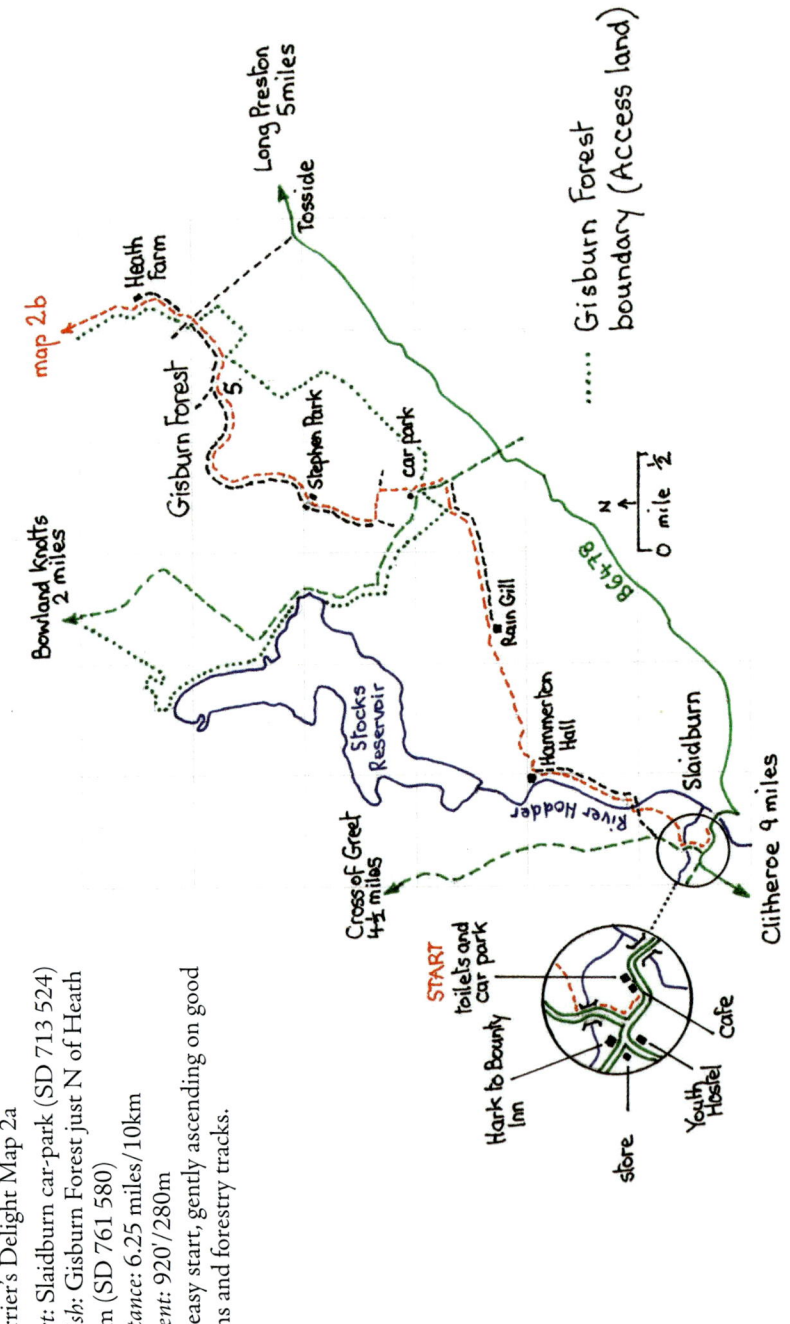

Harrier's Delight Map 2b

Start: Forest just N of Heath Farm (SD 761 580)
Finish: Shooters Clough (SD 660 585)
Distance: 10 miles/16km
Ascent: 1640'/500m

Navigation is easy (mainly following walls and fences) although recent tree felling can sometimes be confusing. On the section between Heath Farm and Cat Knott paths are at best ill-defined and often boggy.

Harrier's Delight Map 2c

Start: Shooters Clough (SD 660 585)
Finish: Whitendale (SD 660 550)

Distance:
18.75 miles/
30.3km

Ascent:
2560'/780m
Brown Syke
to Ward's Stone
is a serious
bog trot.

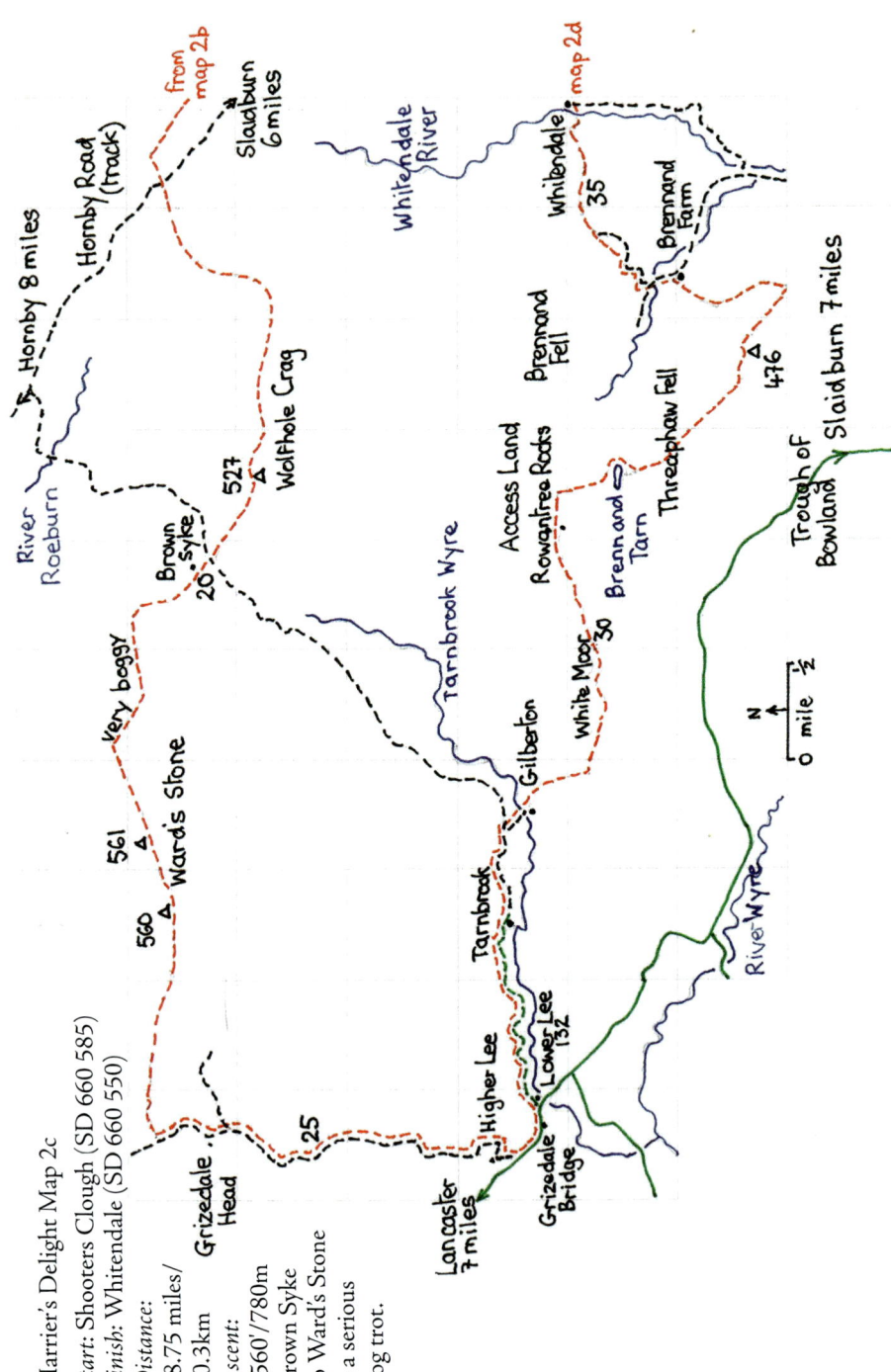

To Hornby 8 miles

River Roeburn

Hornby Road (track)

from map 2b

Sladburn 6 miles

Whitendale River

Whitendale

map 2d

35

Brennand Farm

Wolfhole Crag

527 △

Brown Syke
20

Very boggy

561 △   560 △
Ward's Stone

Tarnbrook Wyre

Brennand Fell

Access Land
Rowantree Rocks

Brennand Tarn

Threaphaw Fell

476 △

Trough of Bowland

Slaidburn 7 miles

White Moor
30

Gilberton

Tarnbrook

River Wyre

N
0   ½   1 mile

Higher Lee

Lower Lee
132

Grizedale Bridge

Grizedale Head

25

Lancaster 7 miles

29

Harrier's Delight Map 2d

Start: Whitendale (SD 660 550)
Finish: Slaidburn car-park (SD 713 524)
Distance: 5.25 miles/8.3km
Ascent: 880′/270m

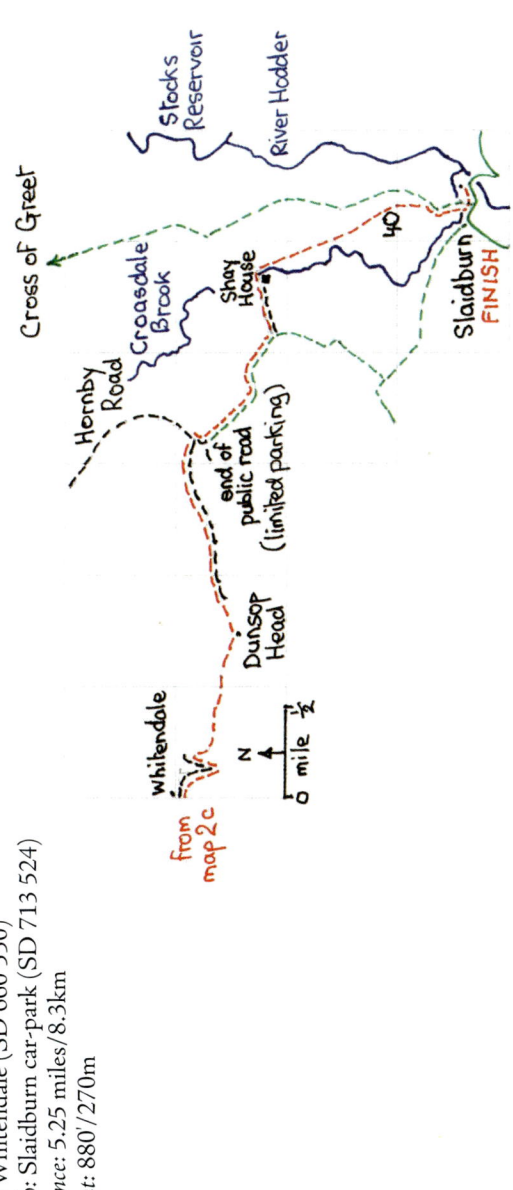

Harrier's Delight Summary

A traditional yomp over the once forbidden and still rarely visited Forest of Bowland.

Apart from Slaidburn there are no shops and no obvious sources of clean water on this remote circular walk.

There are three escape routes back to Slaidburn: the road S from Bowland Knotts; the road S from the Cross of Greet, and the track (Hornby Road) SE from beyond White Hill.

Highest point: Ward's Stone 1840′/561m
Lowest point: Lower Lee 433′/132m

3 The Cumbrian Watershed

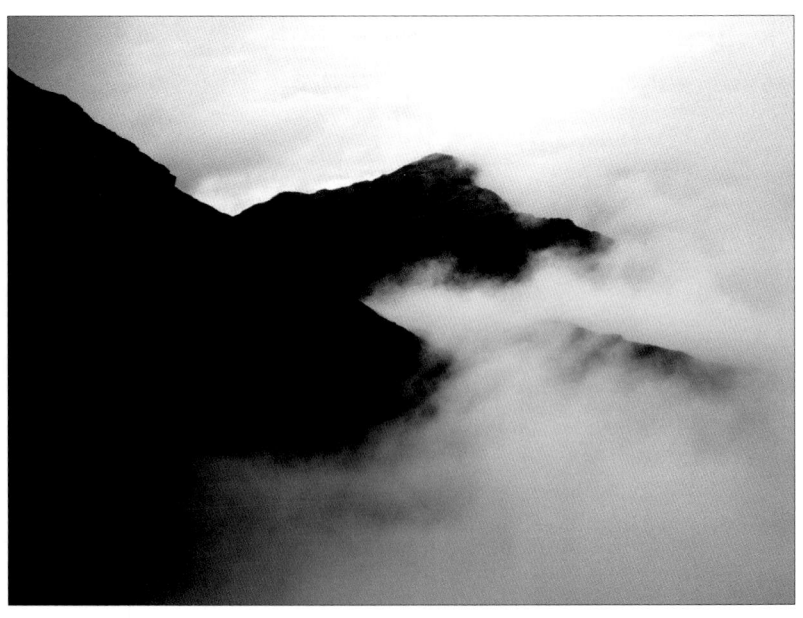

Wetherlam from the slopes of Coniston Old Man

3 The Cumbrian Watershed

Distance: 42.25 miles/68km
Ascent: 14,420'/4395m
Start: Coniston car-park
(SD 303 975)
Finish: Caldbeck car-park
(NY 323 398)
Maps: OS Explorer 1:25,000:
OL4, OL5 OL6 & OL7
The English Lakes NW,
NE, SW & SE.
Other maps that cover
part of the route:
BMC 1:40,000 Lake
District; AA 1:25,000
Central Lake District.

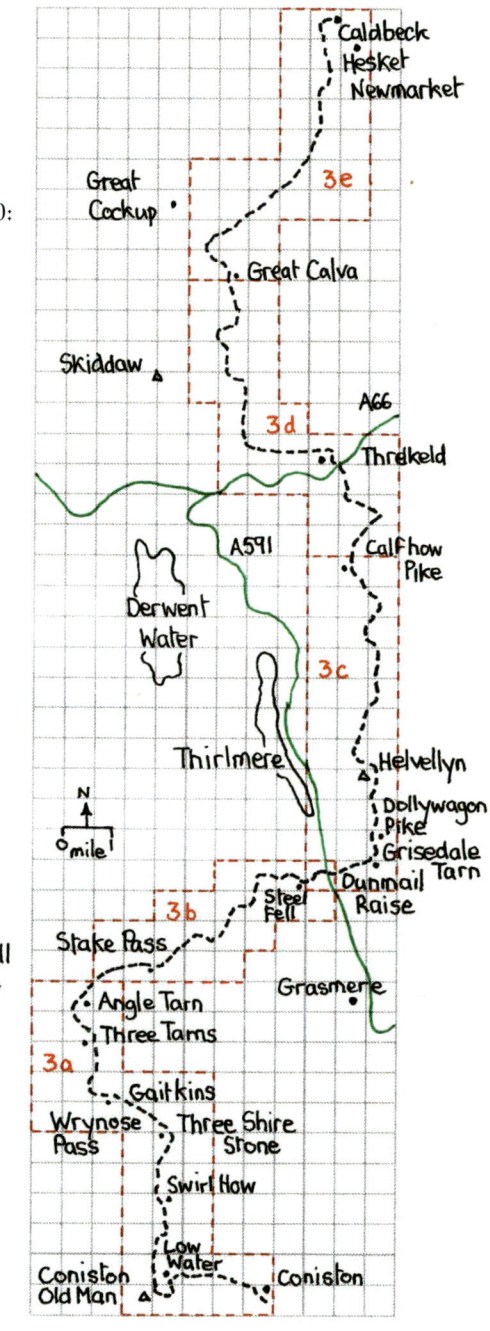

It had long been an ambition of mine to cross the mountains of the Lake District from south to north, a continuous journey that would link my childhood reading of the south Lakes adventures described by Arthur Ransome to the John Peel country that lies 'Back o' Skiddaw'. The opportunity arose when I volunteered to design and complete a sponsored one-day walk/jog from Coniston to Caldbeck. The aim was to keep to the watershed as closely as possible, and include the highest points of the three counties that individually held sway in this proud part of the country. That is, until the gerrymanderers decided to ride roughshod over local sensibilities and rearrange matters for their own Parliamentary purposes.

Although somewhat out on a limb, Coniston village is very much part of Lakeland history. An important centre for lead mining since the reign of Elizabeth I, it began to attract tourists when the railway, originally built to ship the ore, became available to those who could be torn from the fleshpots of Windemere. It eventually gained notoriety through Sir Donald Campbell piloting his craft, Bluebird, to new water-speed records but, long before that, the nearby rock faces of Dow Crag had attracted the attention of climbers. The founding of the renowned Fell & Rock Climbing Club was, in fact, suggested by a group of men employed to design and build ships at the Barrow yards rather than, as is commonly supposed, the gentlemen academics who frequented the hostelry at Wasdale Head.

Our route starts at the village and follows a road to a track that winds its way past Low Water to the summit of the Old Man itself. The term 'Old Man' refers to a mine that has been worked out and reminds us that the Lake District was not invented for the sole purpose of posing for picture postcards. The fells around here are riddled with coffin-shaped tunnels cut to the minimum size to admit a miner and these, with a variety of drains and adits, have formed a hidden world unseen by Google Earth and usually unknown to those who tramp on its surface. Some of these hills are virtually hollow but it is unwise to explore their rickety innards without expert assistance. The mouths of seemingly bottomless pits, excavated to allow water to drain from the workings,

were covered with wooden boards which, now rotten, would be insufficient to bear a man's weight.

But your mind will be on other matters as you traverse the gentle switchback over Swirl How and Great Carrs and make the rather circuitous descent to Wrynose Pass and the Three Shire Stone. The shires in question were Lancashire, Cumberland and Westmoreland. You have topped the first, will pass near the summit of the second and in Helvellyn reach the cairn on the third. But first continue north and by the time you have reached the watershed below Pike of Blisco you will have regained most of the height lost and obtained a clearer idea of what lies ahead. Lurking behind the Langdale Pikes is the next objective, High Raise, and if you were to take a direct route, the distance would be relatively short—a conscientious crow would make little of it. But, as the human blueprint never got round to wings and successive Transport Ministers have yet to come up with the vote-catching wheeze of throwing a suspension bridge across the void, you are in for a detour.

The primary aim of the walk is to keep high and to do this we have to turn sharp left and follow the backbone of a ridge to Bowfell, before sweeping through a gentle chicane to regain our south/north line of travel. Navigation is not as easy as before, particularly over Crinkle Crags where the odd rock impediment tends to bar the way. But it is probably quicker to tackle these head-on and, as it's always a pleasure to use hands as well as feet on a walk, a more satisfying solution than an evasive detour. Although there will not be time on this occasion, the whole of this area is an interesting place to explore. From Gaitkins, the 'corner of the little goats' to the Three Tarns (actually five) hidden in the lee of the aptly named Shelter Crags, there is always something interesting to find and in right conditions the north-facing gullies can offer easy snow and ice climbing until quite late in the winter. I recall an early spring day when I climbed one of these gullies in the morning complete with axe and crampons then, after suitable refreshment at the ODG, spent the afternoon in shirtsleeves on the rock slabs of Gimmer.

It might cross your mind, as you reach the top of Bowfell, that another challenge lies close to the route you have chosen. The same-day ascent of the Lakeland 3000ers is completed by a good

number of people every year and was one of the original mountain challenge walks. If you were to include Scafell and its apparently subsidiary Pike, then pop up Skiddaw as you pass, you will have not only completed the Four Peaks but done something approaching the famous Bob Graham Round (see 'Baggers & Trotters' on p. 121) or, at the very least, a good training run before any such attempt is made. It might be wiser, in that event, to have a good look around on a previous outing as, if speed is of the essence, you will need to have reconnoitred the ground pretty thoroughly.

Scafell Pike is the highest point in England but, unless your idea of a day out is picking your way through orange peel among an assortment of Boy Scouts, reluctant girlfriends and self-appointed local experts, there is not much more to be said for it. Scafell is much the more majestic, with its forbidding cliffs confounding any approach from the east and north. From Mickledore the single point of weakness is where these two cliffs meet but even Broad Stand, the name given to this series of sloping ledges, is still classified in the Fell & Rock guidebooks as a technical rock climb. The route has also gained mythical status as it is reported that the poet Coleridge descended this 'fearsome place' by the simple expedient of hanging by his fingertips from one ledge, then letting go in the hope that through God and good fortune he would land on another. Anyone who has examined the problem would appreciate this differs somewhat from the average textbook advice.

Whichever your decision, you will eventually find yourself perched above Angle Tarn and realise, despite this being the Lake District, it is the first large expanse of water you have actually passed close by since Low Water at the start of the journey. Others have been seen from a distance and, some hundreds of feet below, Thirlmere and Ullswater will march alongside you as you traverse the Helvellyn range, but from now onwards only Grisedale Tarn will be sufficiently adjacent for a convenient paddle.

This is not surprising really, as we are trying to walk the watershed and water tends to run and collect downhill, and it also explains the attraction of the area. Lakeland fells have often been likened to the spokes of a wheel and it is true that's how they appear on the map. On the ground they more resemble an

irregularly squashed limpet with a variety of rock pools trapped in its misshapen hollows. As a result of this configuration, there are always pleasing glimpses of water reflecting fell and rock. This combination, set against swards of close-cropped pasture (courtesy of that state-subsidised lawnmower, the Herdwick sheep), goes a long way to explain the District's particular charm.

The section from Stake Pass to Dunmail Raise is one of the less distinct and, some may say, distinguished parts of the Lakes. As it does not offer an obvious way from or to somewhere of note, there are few well-trodden paths and a little care is needed to find the most suitable way to the road crossing. The most sensible idea is to aim for the summit of Steel Fell which is the best launchpad for a knee-wrecking descent of 500 or so feet to the road that joins Ambleside to Keswick. Rather than picking your way gingerly over the rough steep terrain, it is probably best to get it over and done with—the experienced fell-runner flies down such slopes in a series of ten-foot bounds—but it should be pointed out that if you aim to make your descent in 50 steps, it would be best to get some practice in first. As compensation for the pain, you have less feet to reclimb on your way to Grisedale Tarn and the foot of Dollywagon Pike.

The ridge above culminates in the Lake District's third highest peak and one-time County Top of Westmoreland. 'The pale yellow moorland' is one of the most popular mountains in Britain and with good reason. It is easy of access, particularly from the west, and the deep valleys that contain Thirlmere and Ullswater sufficiently separate the ridge from its neighbouring peaks to allow extensive views in all directions. Sightseers and tourists have tramped or been taken there by pony for more than two centuries and for many aspiring fell-walkers Helvellyn was his or her first real mountain.

What is surprising, given such popularity, is the sparseness of the summit furniture. Unlike some that are crowned with a variety of edifice that in other circumstances would have demanded planning permission, the plateau that holds the highest point has little in the way of ornamentation. An undistinguished pile of stones marks the top and a windbreak in the form of a cross offers the minimum of shelter. But what it lacks in architectural ambition it more than makes up for in memorial display. Just below the

summit is a stone marking the death of a foxhunter and on the plateau itself a tablet commemorates the arrival and departure of an aeroplane. This feat was performed by one Bert Hinkler, a test pilot for A V Roe. He apparently had little difficulty in landing into the wind, but his take-off was somewhat more exciting as, unable to gather sufficient airspeed, the biplane effectively fell over the edge of a cliff where, thanks to the beneficence of gravity, it gained enough momentum to avoid crashing into Striding Edge.

The most renowned memorial, however, is to Foxie, the 'one faithful friend' of the artist Charles Gough. After his master had slipped and fallen to his death she remained by his side until, three months later, the body with the dog still in attendance was discovered by a local shepherd. The story caught the imagination of the public in general and the artistic and literary world in particular. The artist, Landseer, produced a suitably sentimental portrait and both Sir Walter Scott and Wordsworth put pen to paper to create, as the latter put it, a 'lasting monument of words'. By the time Gough's body was discovered it was a virtual skeleton. The romantics, unwilling to spoil a good story, had it scavenged by ravens—the sceptics might have questioned how the faithful friend had survived so long.

What follows is one of the easier sections of high-level walking you can hope to encounter and the summits roll under your feet as easily as they roll off the tongue, Nethermost, Helvellyn, a collection of Dodds, until finally Calfhow Pike has you looking down the track of your third and final descent. Rights of way lead you through burgeoning habitation before you eventually reach Threlkeld. As the inn sign suggests, you are now at the edge of John Peel country. To the minds of many, this figure epitomises the jolly Lakeland huntsman who adorns prints and pubs. The truth is, Peel was far from 'jolly', choosing to impoverish his family rather than sacrifice his own pleasure. Nor was he a true Lakelander but hunted exclusively in the northern Cumbrian flatlands south of Carlisle. Moreover, on horseback, rather than following the fox on foot, as was usual in the much rougher country further south.

From Threlkeld, there is a well-constructed track leading to Skiddaw House and if the Scafells were included in your itinerary the time has come for you to consider whether you have sufficient

energy to contemplate an ascent of Skiddaw ('popping up' will now appear a touch optimistic), thus completing the round of the Big Four. Mind you, it doesn't pay to be too complacent about the Lakeland Fells, particularly on the flanks facing north or east. I recall, in preparation for an attempt on the Bob Graham Round, crossing from Skiddaw to Great Calva in running shoes. It wasn't the depths of winter but the temperature had dropped and the wind was coming in from the north east. It wasn't long before I realised that running shoes and ice don't mix. Panic set in. The flanks of nearby Great Cockup Fell raised a knowing eyebrow. But, as they say, 'When you gotta go, you gotta go' and I did, towards a rather substantial-looking stone wall. As luck would have it, an accumulation of old snow remained in the wall's lee, which sufficiently slowed my involuntary version of the Cresta Run and enabled a fending off of the obstacle without breaking my wrists. To the casual spectator it probably appeared that I was in total control. The inner man knew otherwise.

Once you have reached the summit of Great Calva, you can be assured there is no more serious 'up' and you are on your final section of what has been for the most part a ridge walk rather than a roller coaster. You may be surprised to discover from the summit of Knott that one of the bypassable bumps again turns out to be Scafell (or, a little optimistically, Great Sca Fell) and, as you continue, it may cross your mind to devise a series of walks joining two peaks in the Lakes that share a common name. Other than the Scafells, and unlike the plethora of Big, Red, Black and White Bens in Scotland, only the combination of Red Pike, Buttermere and Red Pike, Wasdale readily springs to mind, but I suspect with a fairly close study of the relevant OS maps quite a decent list could be made. At the very least, it could occupy your thoughts over the wet winter evenings.

All in all, the Back o' Skiddaw is a curious corner of the Lakes. A little off-route lies Carrock Fell, which offers the only bit of sustained rock climbing on gabbro outside the Skye Ridge. This is one of the results of a titanic collision in this part of the world during which various strata of rocks came to a grinding halt. The resultant fells, thrust into space to fill the gap between

the beginnings and ends of our journey, now come to a halt with remarkable abruptness and the rest of Cumbria rolls out bucolically towards the Scottish Border. We are beyond the Lake District as the Tourist Board knows it and there is a feeling that this part of the world has not changed much as time moved past. A pub like The Old Crown at Hesket Newmarket, with its own brewery round the back producing ales with tempting names like Blencathra and Skiddaw, seems more to reflect real Lakeland than the fleshpot Slugs and Lettuces with their lagers and alcopops.

After leaving the cairn of High Pike and as you meander downhill past the hamlet of Nether Row, you could mentally tick off the number of Wainwright summits you have climbed. You will probably feel quite pleased with yourself, but best not get too carried away. Joss Naylor once did 30+ Wainwrights a day, seven days on the trot. When you arrive at Caldbeck you could well drop into the Oddfellows Arms, which is fitting enough, as people who choose to wander the length of a National Park, adding a stone to every summit cairn they pass, would probably not be regarded as run-of-the-mill.

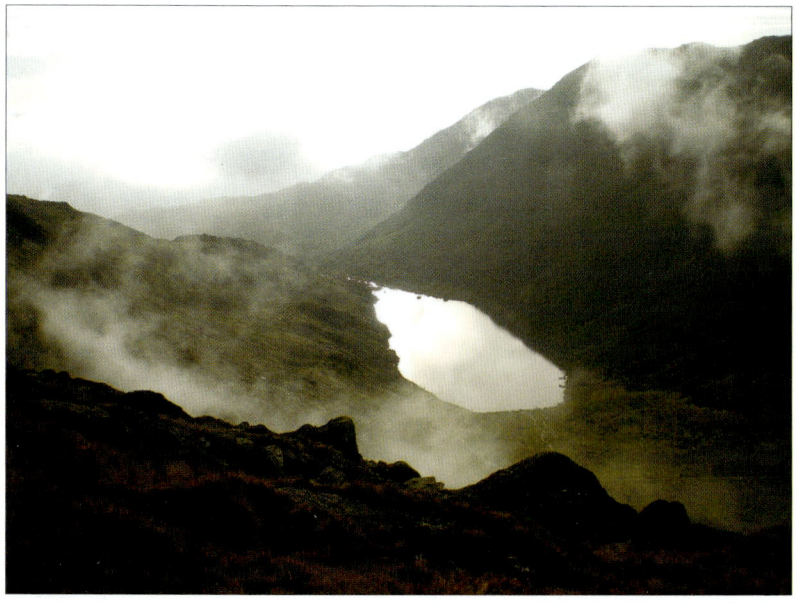

Goat's Water and Dow Crag

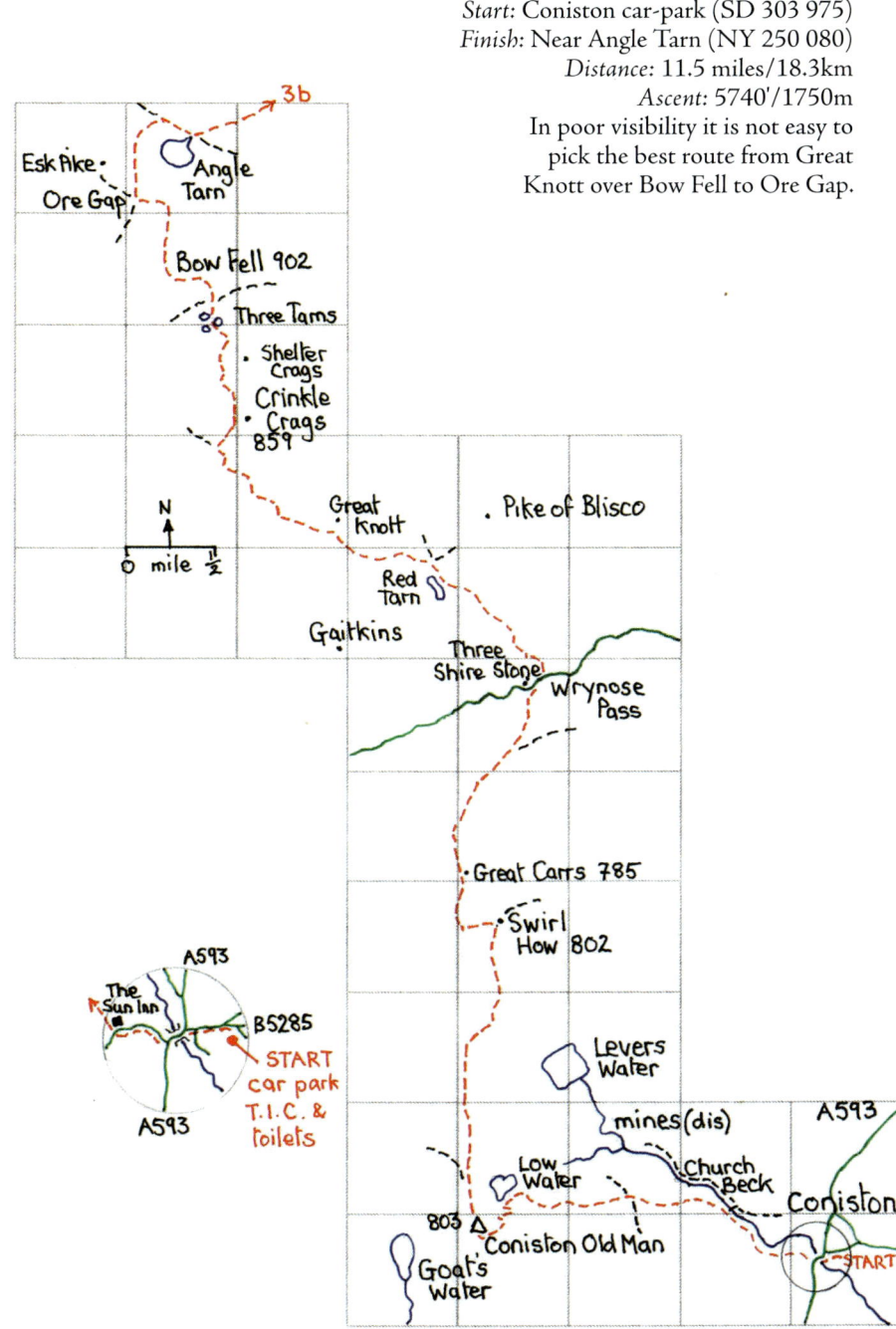

The Cumbrian Watershed Map 3a
Start: Coniston car-park (SD 303 975)
Finish: Near Angle Tarn (NY 250 080)
Distance: 11.5 miles/18.3km
Ascent: 5740'/1750m
In poor visibility it is not easy to
pick the best route from Great
Knott over Bow Fell to Ore Gap.

3b

Esk Pike
Ore Gap
Angle Tarn

Bow Fell 902

Three Tarns

Shelter Crags
Crinkle Crags 859

N

0 mile ½

Great Knott

Pike of Blisco

Red Tarn

Gaitkins

Three Shire Stone

Wrynose Pass

Great Carrs 785

Swirl How 802

A593
The Sun Inn
B5285
START
car park
T.I.C. &
toilets
A593

Levers Water

mines (dis)

A593

Church Beck

Coniston

803 △
Low Water
Coniston Old Man

Goat's Water

START

40

The Cumbrian Watershed Map 3b

Start: Near Angle Tarn (NY 250 080)
Finish: Dunmail Raise A591 (NY327 117)
Distance: 6.5 miles/10.6km
Ascent: 1590'/484m

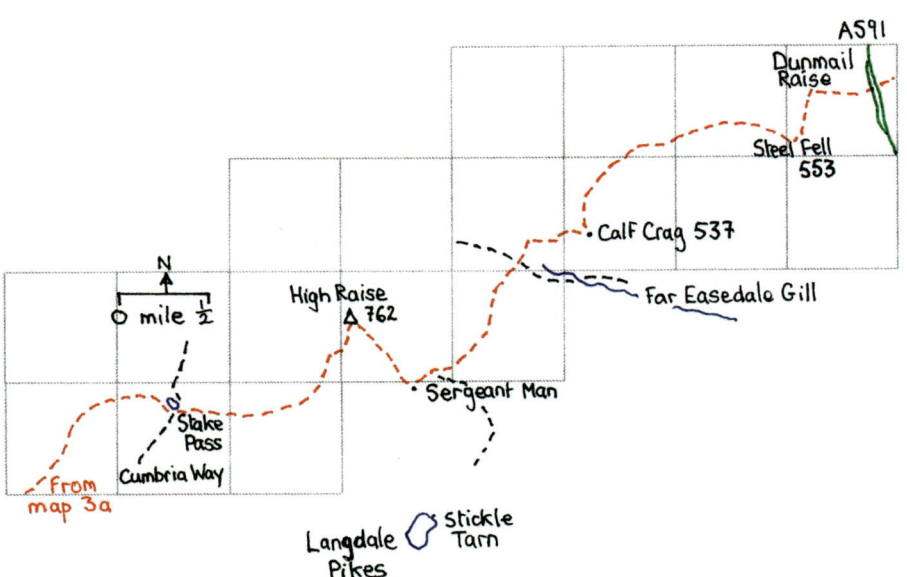

The Cumbrian Watershed Map 3c
Start: Dunmail Raise A591
(NY 327 117)
Finish: Just S of Clough Head
(NY 332 220)
Distance: 8.75 miles/14km
Ascent: 3810'/1162m

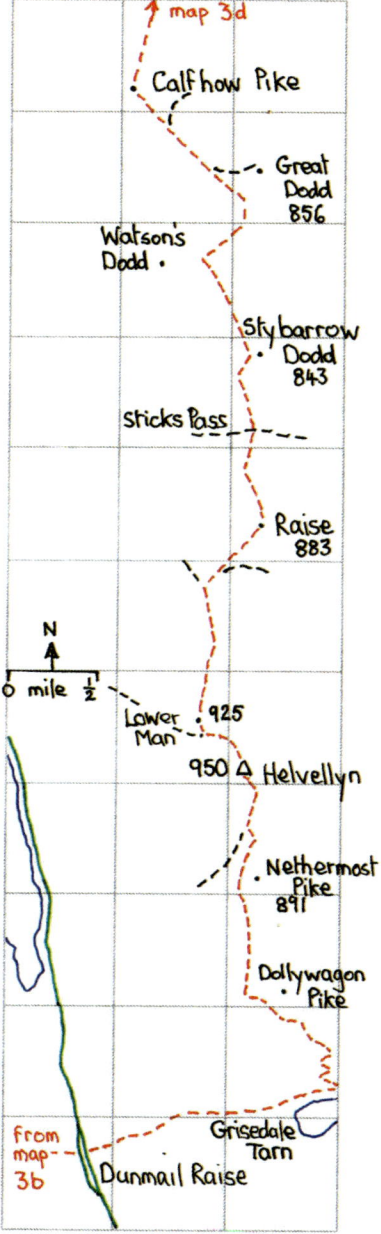

map 3d

Calf how Pike

Great Dodd 856

Watson's Dodd .

Stybarrow Dodd 843

Sticks Pass

Raise 883

N

0 mile ½

Lower Man . 925

950 △ Helvellyn

. Nethermost Pike 891

Dollywagon . Pike

Grisedale Tarn

from map 3b

Dunmail Raise

The Cumbrian Watershed Map 3d

Start: Just S of Clough Head (NY 332 220)
Finish: Great Calva (NY 290 306)
Distance: 8.25 miles/13.3km
Ascent: 2320'/707m

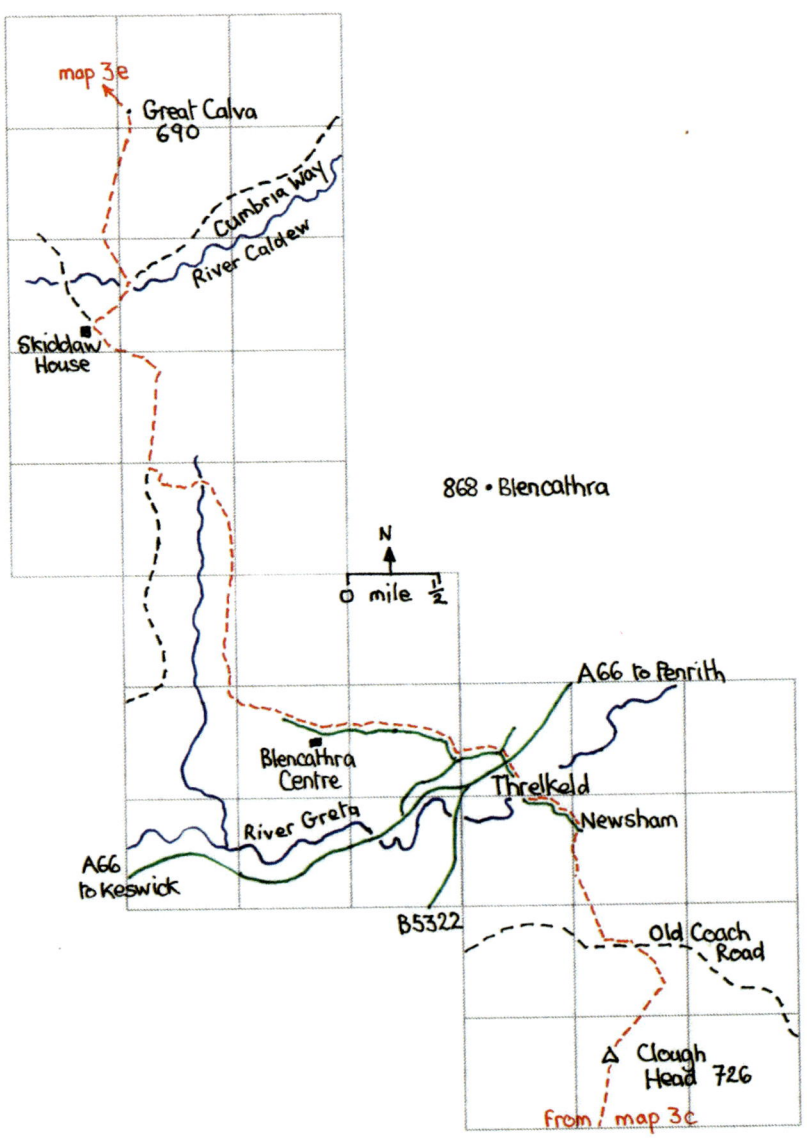

The Cumbrian Watershed Map 3e

Start: Great Calva (NY 290 306)
Finish: Caldbeck car-park
(NY 323 398)
Distance: 7.25 miles/11.8km
Ascent: 960'/292m

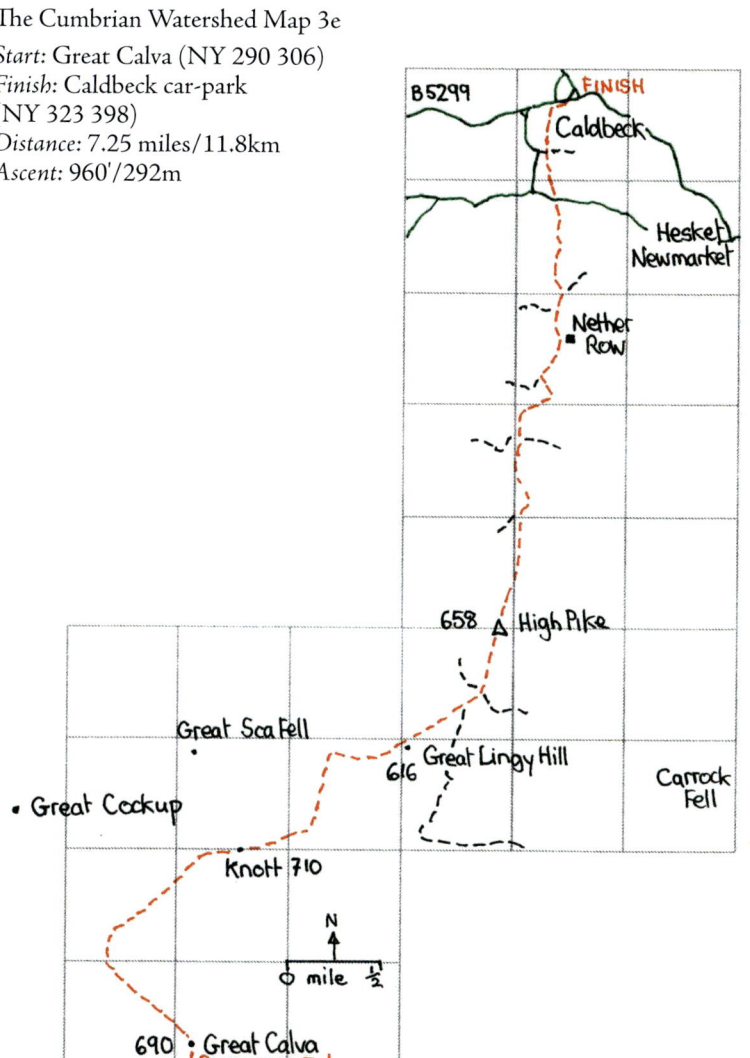

The Cumbrian Watershed Summary

A high-level traverse of the Lakeland fells, taking in the former county tops of Lancashire, Cumberland and Westmoreland. This linear route crosses the A591 and A66, and hence bus routes to Keswick, Ambleside and links to Coniston. Buses to Keswick or Carlisle from the finish at Caldbeck are very infrequent.

Highest point: Helvellyn 3117'/950m
Lowest point: Coniston 171'/52m

4 A Bridge Far Enough

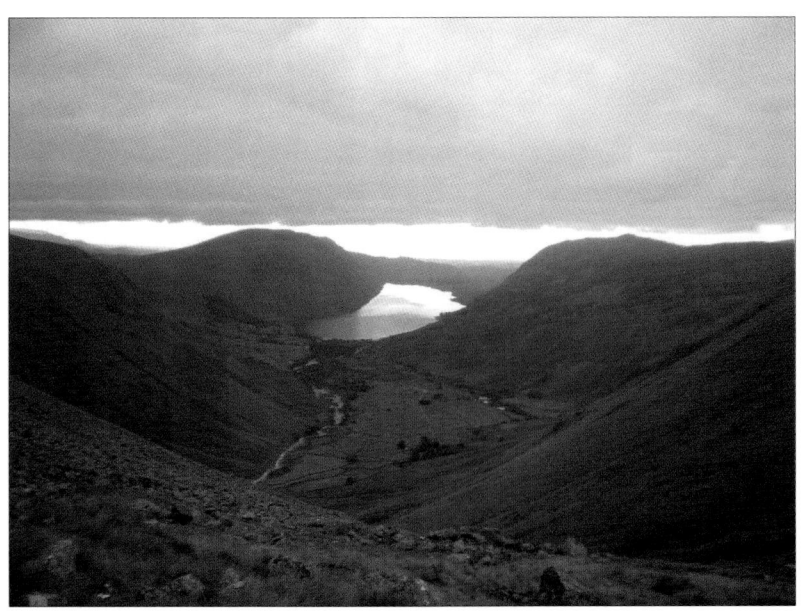

Wast Water from the Climbers' Traverse

4 A Bridge Far Enough

Distance: 42 miles/67.3km

Ascent: 13,460'/4104m

Start: Ennerdale Bridge (NY 069 158)

Finish: Garnett Bridge (SD 523 993)

Maps: OS Explorer 1:25,000: OL4, OL5, OL6 & OL7 The English Lakes NW, NE, SW & SE; other maps that cover part of the route: BMC 1:40,000 Lake District; AA 1:25,000 Central Lake District; A-Z 1:25,000 Lake District Northern Fells & Southern Fells.

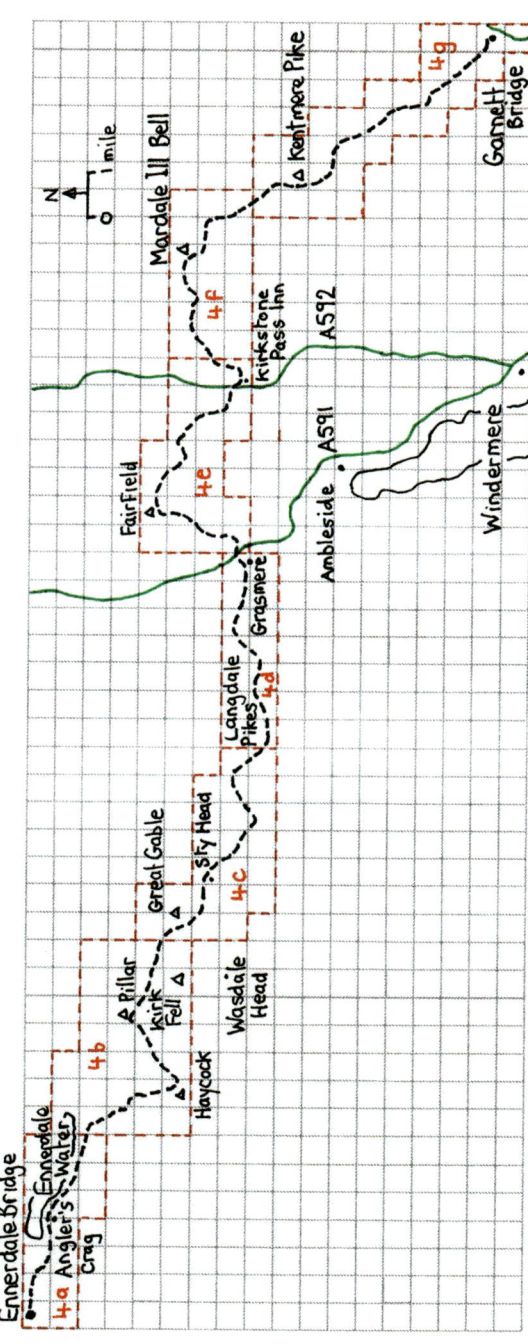

There is something satisfactory about a route that starts and ends at a bridge. A clear sense of a beginning and an end, the alpha and omega of it, so to speak. The Bridges in this case are Ennerdale in the west and Garnett in the east and they act not only like brackets enclosing the great central fells but also serve to introduce both a sense of mounting expectation as you approach the initial slopes and a note of quiet satisfaction as, hours later, you slide into the final valley. This route differs from the previously described north/south route, as the latter keeps to the watershed, only begrudgingly losing height where roads have to be crossed. Navigation of the Cumbrian Watershed is simple—just keep to the highest bits available—whereas our present Lakeland route tends to run against the grain and is forced to swoop and leap through the valleys, ducking and diving to make the best of the available ground.

As with Wainwright's Coast to Coast, a decision has to be made about the direction of travel. I have chosen west to east. Not only for the pragmatic reason that you will have the elements at your back but also, if you are lucky with the weather, the pleasure of watching shadows lengthen and the setting sun throw the afternoon fells into ever-sharpening relief. But whichever your choice, the route has the particular virtues of crossing some of the least visited parts of the Lake District. As only the A591 and its off-shoot the A592 bisect the high fells, and as both are within easy reach of the M6, cars and their occupants tend to collect around the likes of Ambleside, Grasmere and Keswick. The further you move away from these honeypots, the less of a crowd you are likely to see.

From Ennerdale Bridge, which is about as far away as you can get, you should step out into comparative peace and quiet and start the walk along a path that, running under Angler's Crag, follows the valley, before swinging at lake's end up the fellside. The higher you get, the more forest is seen below, sweeping up the dale to the headwall of Wind Gap. The plantation was part of a post World War One initiative to ensure Britain was capable of producing all the timber it needed and so not be reliant on easily ambushed overseas supplies. The trees planted were in the main Norwegian

and Sitka Spruce, an ideal wood for the pitprops on which so much of the energy supplies literally rested. As you might expect from a Government Agency, the trees were planted in regimental lines, creating, as they marched up the valley, rank upon rank of dreary orthodoxy.

Immediately there was an outcry. Whether the military precision struck an unhappy chord or the harsh lines contrasted so unfavourably with the gentler folds of the surrounding fells is difficult to say, but I suspect a certain amount of collective nimbyism was, and still is, at work. The objectors should remember that the Lake District they love has also been caused by man's planning and if they want matters to remain in their natural state, they would also have to accept their beloved hills covered with overgrown scrub. Moreover, I suspect they would be the first to squeak if a flick of the electric light switch does not produce the required effect. My own objection is not against plantations *per se*—with suitable broad-leaf intrusion and irregular planting they can be made relatively attractive—but more the timing of such political decisions, which appear to be reactive rather than proactive.

For it is not only forestry but also the management of a whole range of natural resources that should concern us all. The sound of stable doors slamming throughout government offices around the globe must be sufficient to awaken the dead. Except there lies the rub. When finite resources have gone, there can be no resurrection. It may be that man's ingenuity will prevail, but it seems a long shot when placed against the demands of an ever-increasing population. The simple answer would be for the world's leaders to gather, forget their ambitions for re-election and agree to place what remains in a world resource bank, then administer it for the benefit of humanity as a whole. I expect by now, in your mind's eye, you are already seeing the pigs taxiing down the runway, yet in the end it is only a matter of mindset. It must start somewhere. As individuals who take pleasure out of the countryside, we have a responsibility to take the lead in saving it.

Once you have reached the lip of the ridge just below Haycock and lost sight of the trees of Ennerdale, you set foot on a circuit

of one of the grandest of Lakeland dales and, when it comes to mountaineering, one of the most historically important. If the hollow combe of Wasdale was the cradle of rock climbing in Britain, then the hotel at Wasdale Head was the font at which it was blessed. Here, in the nineteenth century, university reading parties gathered to study the works of Homer and Virgil against a suitably inspirational background. Steeple and Pillar, the names of the fells now standing before you, have a sense of ecclesiastical loftiness that well suited the muscular Christianity of the young men studying the storming of the walls of Troy with one part of their mind and planning a similar assault on the ramparts of Gable and Scafell with another.

For some it was more the challenge of the Grandes Jorasses than of the 'Greats' of final examinations that turned their eyes from the page towards the surrounding hills. If Easter was early and the snow had lingered, they could get into shape for their trips to Zermatt and Chamonix the following summer. The deep gullies would offer the chance to polish their snow and ice work and the adjoining ridges could present technical challenges that were the equal of anything they might tackle in the Alps. Yet of all the would-be lawyers, bishops and cabinet ministers, there was one young man whose eyes most strayed from his studies. W P Haskett Smith was studying law, and indeed became a barrister, but he is not remembered for his toils among the inextricabilities of Equity and the Common Law, rather as the Father of Rock Climbing in the British Isles.

And now as we continue along the ridge over Steeple and Pillar Fell, we approach one of his earliest stamping grounds. Pillar Rock lies a few hundred feet below the Fell's trig point and is, in my opinion at least, the finest chunk of stone south of the Border. Other cliffs have faces that are higher and wider but, for the most part, lean flat against the parent mountain. Pillar is three dimensional and all four faces are impenetrable to the ordinary walker. There are easy enough ways to the top, but none so easy that it would be advisable to lean backwards and let go. And that was exactly the situation Haskett Smith experienced during an early attempt of the longest ridge on the north face.

He had reached a point where the difficulties forced him to retreat by sliding gingerly down a large chunk of rock that lay against the main face. As he shifted his weight, he felt the block move and realised that the huge boulder, far from being firmly grounded on a supporting ledge, was precariously balanced on its fulcrum. For what seemed an age he remained bound to the block like some classical hero of his studies but, forced to act, this modern-day Prometheus managed to find a left handhold that was attached to the solid cliff face and, at one and the same time, swung his weight free, using his right hand and a flailing boot to dispatch the rock into the valley below.

Haskett Smith's trials on the North Climb were part of a deliberate attempt to seek out difficulty for its own sake, but for generations before him Pillar Rock was thought inaccessible and the early guidebook writers issued suitably dire warnings of its perils. Nonetheless, the summit was finally reached when the *Cumberland Advertiser* notified its readers that, on 9th July 1826, John Atkinson of Cockermouth had set foot on its top. Since then hundreds if not thousands of ascents have been made and, in retrospect, I am delighted that my first real rock climb was on the west face of Pillar. Although I have climbed on most major cliffs in Britain, and felt a greater satisfaction on completing climbs that were technically more difficult or potentially more dangerous, I have never felt the same sense of fulfilment as I did more than half a century ago when I pulled over the final handholds of The New West and saw I was on the top.

But our route can afford no such diversion as our next objective, the crossroads of Sty Head, lies two miles to the east with the imposing bulks of Kirk Fell and Great Gable standing firmly in our way. Fortunately, the concerted efforts of sheep and man have made the passage considerably easier. From Black Sail, the pass between Ennerdale and Wasdale, you can skirt Kirk Fell by a well-worn path to reach the flanks of Great Gable and join Moses' Trod, an old through-route connecting Honister and Wasdale. Here a decision awaits—to go up or around? For many walkers, the summit is all and their arrival heralds, if not a blast of triumphal trumpets, at least the moment for a ceremonial unpacking of

the sandwiches. I am not so sure. I admit to acknowledging my arrival at various summit cairns with an apparently affectionate tap of the boot, but this usually signals less the achievement, more the anticipation of the knee-wrecking descent to come.

Unless you are on a ridge of Cuillin proportions, the view is often disappointing. A summit plateau can obscure rather than reveal and it is only when you start to descend that any vista unfolds. My ideal viewpoint is from a high-level traverse with an unimpeded sight of the valley below. To me, it is the difference between climbing out of a trapdoor in the middle of a flat roof and reaching the same place by the exterior fire-escape. It is, therefore, not surprising that I consider the next section as one of the best pieces of rough walking in the Lake District. The Climbers' Traverse, for it is man who has fashioned this track of rock steps and surprise views, runs beneath the crags and scree slopes of the south face of Great Gable.

As the name suggests, the route passes the ridges and chimneys that offered ideal climbing for the early habitués of the Wastwater Hotel and I am sure most would agree this particular traverse is certainly better than some tiresome plod up a featureless hillside. For a start, here is curious rock architecture to catch your interest: Sphinx Rock, which from a certain angle has all the enigmatic quality of the original, the queerly shaped Bear Rock, described by Haskett Smith as 'difficult to find, especially when the grass is long' and, most famously of all, the totemic Napes Needle, first climbed by the same man in 1879. But today the likes of Arrowhead Ridge and Eagle's Nest Direct mostly lie silent. To the modern climber they are too easy and an unnecessarily long walk from the car, with a serious risk of getting wet. It seems to me popular climbing has succumbed to some law of diminishing returns. Where once icy heights were scaled, now it's indoor climbing walls with an ambient temperature of 16 Celsius.

The Traverse wends its way under Kern Knotts to reach Sty Head and the box housing the Mountain Rescue kit. This spot is, in many ways, the Piccadilly Circus of the Lake District, the point where paths from Ennerdale, Borrowdale, Langdale and Wasdale finally converge. So crucial is this pass that it sparked, in the late

nineteenth century, a proposal by Keswick Urban District Council to construct a road which would connect Keswick with Wasdale. The proposal was seconded by a Mr Musgrave, who suggested the project would be 'an admirable way of celebrating the Queen's extraordinary reign'. Whether this commendable outburst of patriotic zeal was in any way connected with his recent purchase of an interest in a nearby hostelry is not recorded. Fortunately, wiser counsels and Councils prevailed.

Once Sty Head has been reached, you will most probably meet the traffic that has gathered for the final assault on the summit of England's highest mountain. On a Bank Holiday Monday it can come as a bit of a shock and reminds me of my first visit to the city of Worcester. At one point the motorist approaches a rather confusing offset series of junctions remarkable for an absence of lights or roundabouts. With high-speed traffic arriving from all directions, I was confronted by a sign bearing the instruction MERGE AND WEAVE. I can only suggest that, between Sty Head and Esk Hause, you adopt similar tactics, secure in the knowledge that once Ore Gap is passed, you can slip behind Rossett Pike and, unmolested, speed through the hinterland that lies behind the Langdale Pikes and Pavey Ark. It is then a matter of holding your best height before dropping into Easdale and the village of Grasmere.

This must be one of the most pleasant villages in the Lake District and it has to be said Wordsworth chose well. So, unfortunately for the misanthropes who have to pass through it, did several others. If Sty Head is Camp IV, then the likes of Grasmere and Ambleside are something approaching Kathmandu. But fortunately, as far as Kathmandus go, Grasmere is somewhat smaller in scale and it will not be long before you are looking down on the 'famous Swan'. It is at this point you realise that this is one of those troughs mentioned in the opening paragraph and there's a resultant steep pull before we arrive at the ridge leading to Great Rigg and Rydal Head. But, as is so often the case in the Lakes, after the ascent comes the reward and a pleasant ridge walk follows. with fine views towards Brothers Water and Patterdale. It will not be long, however, before you have reached Scandale Pass

and start the shorter descent past the steeple-shaped stone that gives Kirkstone Pass its name.

There are certain locations that are stamped forever in your mind, not because of their position or exceptional beauty but because of an event. Such, for me, is the Kirkstone Inn. Many years ago, I had followed the just-described route from Grasmere and decided that the inn could offer a pleasant interlude before my ascent onto High Street. The bar was empty save for a young barmaid. The time was around midday. I went through the usual formalities—approached the bar, placed my order and waited in anticipation. Nothing happened. I tried again. Not a flicker of reaction. I considered the options. It had been raining, the ground was muddy and a slip on Red Screes had not enhanced my already dubious sartorial splendour. Perhaps she thought I was a tramp. To reassure her, I somewhat ostentatiously took a five-pound note out of my pocket. The effect was instantaneous. She burst into tears and fled. I was about to leave when the landlord appeared. Apparently, the barmaid had just heard an announcement on the radio that Elvis had died.

And then there are some locations, no matter how many times they've been visited, that fail to stick in my mind. The eastern fells, at large, fall into this category. I know them well enough. I have even walked from Kentmere to Penrith along the full length of High Street and more than once from Patterdale to Shap, yet I still find it difficult to nudge sharp images from the edges of my memory. Perhaps, it's all a matter of topography. Now that we are in the old county of Westmoreland, the landscape has changed. No longer do the high mountains harbour looming cliffs, slabs of grey rock buttressing their summits, or offer striking Napes Needles or climbers' hotels, reminders of former mounting ambition. Here the fells are less shapely, the ghylls more prosaic.

Not that this is necessarily a complaint. It has its own character, somewhat detached from the hubble and bubble of more popular fells. Once you have reached the likes of Mardale Ill Bell and Nan Bield Pass, you meet not people but ghosts—of Roman centurions patrolling their beat along their ancient ways, wild ponies and the gypsies who rode them, the villagers of Measand and Mardale

Green, sacrificed to satisfy Manchester's need for clean water. Or, circling high above you, a pair of golden eagles trying to establish a toehold south of the Border. Once Kentmere Pike is safely passed, your thoughts can turn to home, secure in the knowledge you have nearly walked from one side of the National Park to the other. Below Shipman Knotts a good track leads into Longsleddale and the banks of the River Sprint, though raising one is probably the last thing on your mind. Rather, at this stage of the day, you should hope for a fine summer's evening and a leisurely stroll along the riverside path. Then, at the last, await your lift, leaning hands outspread, on the warm grey stone of Garnett Bridge.

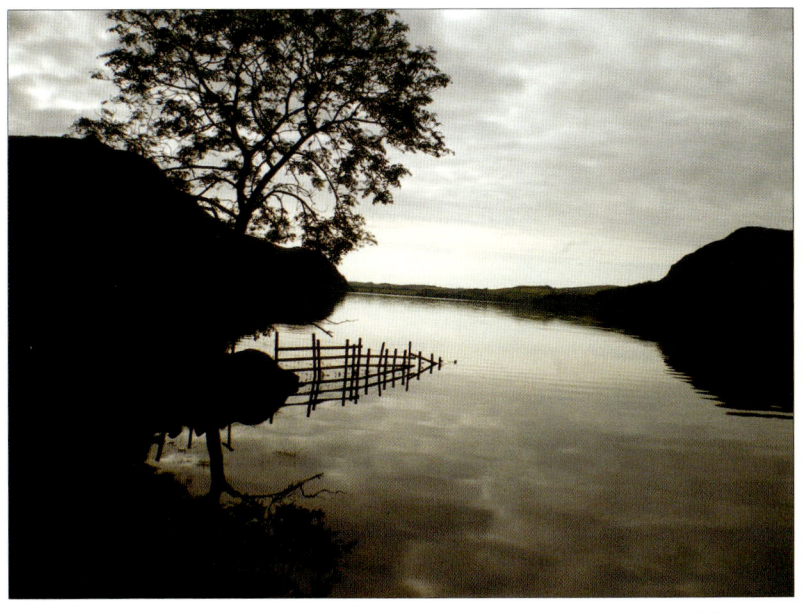

Ennerdale Water

A Bridge Far Enough Map 4a
Start: Ennerdale Bridge (NY 069 158)
Finish: Track at E end of Ennerdale Water (NY 103 138)
Distance: 4.25 miles/7km
Ascent: 210'/65m

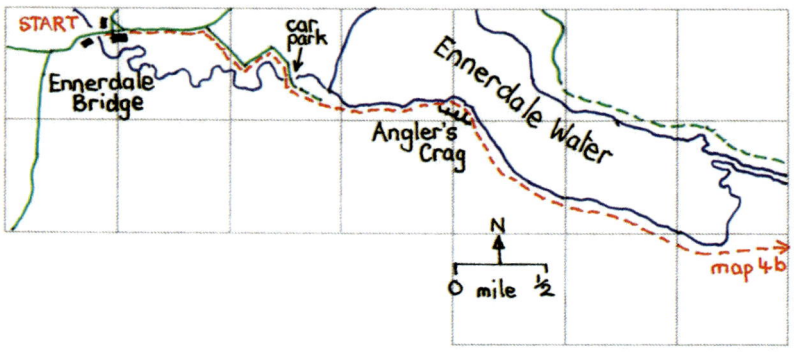

A Bridge Far Enough Map 4b
Start: Track at E end of Ennerdale Water (NY 103 138)
Finish: Boat How (NY 200 112)
Distance: 6 miles/9.6km
Ascent: 3470'/1058m

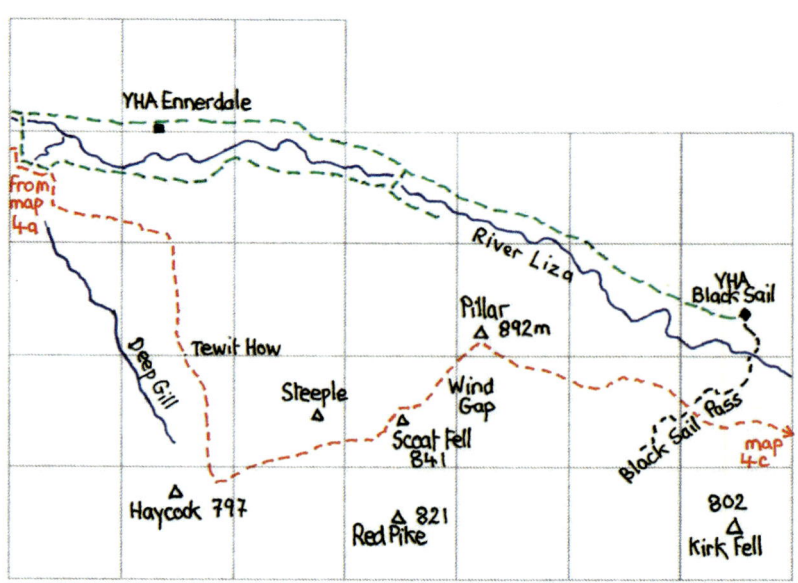

55

A Bridge Far Enough Map 4c

Start: Boat How (NY 200 112)
Finish: Martcrag Moor (NY 268 080)
Distance: 6 miles/9.7km
Ascent: 1970'/600m

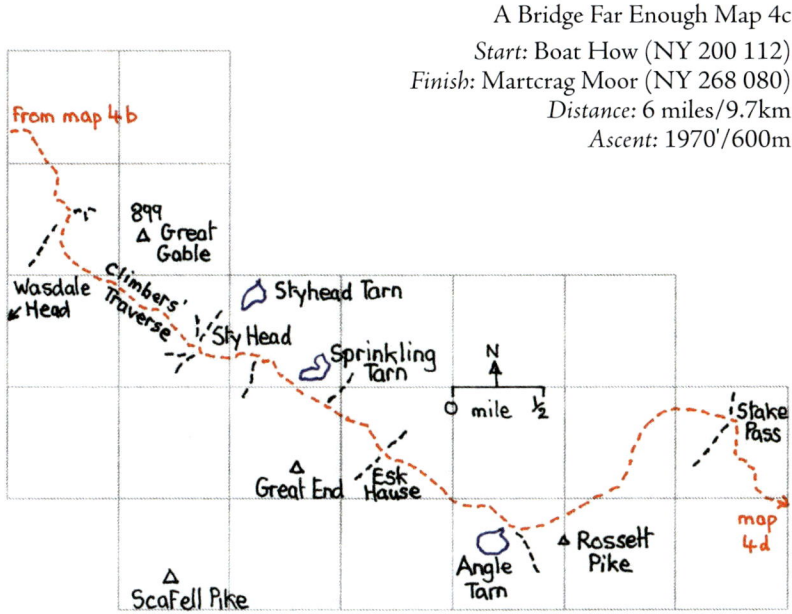

A Bridge Far Enough Map 4d

Start: Martcrag Moor (NY 268 080)
Finish: Grasmere A591 (NY 340 082)
Distance: 5.5 miles/8.8km
Ascent: 1030'/314m

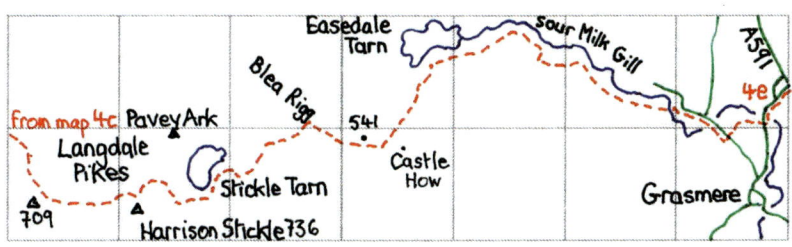

A Bridge Far Enough Map 4e

Start: Grasmere A591 (NY 340 082)
Finish: Pike How (NY 410 090)
Distance: 7.5 miles/11.9km
Ascent: 4540'/1384m

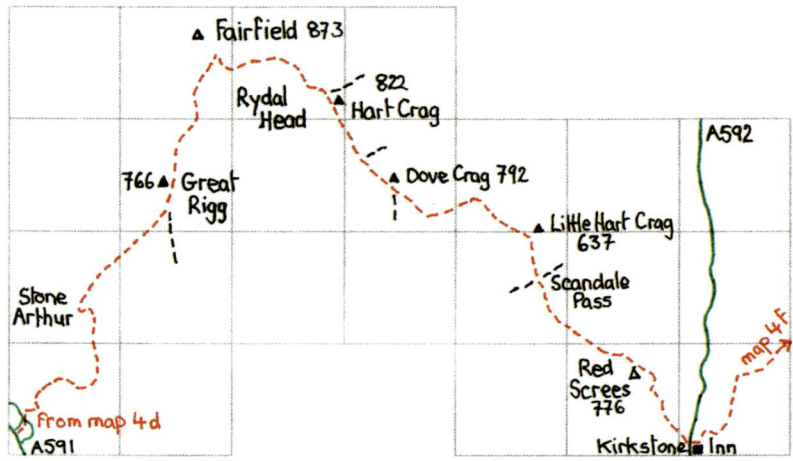

A Bridge Far Enough Map 4f

Start: Pike How (NY 410 090)
Finish: Col just N of Kentmere Pike (NY 463 080)
Distance: 5 miles/7.9km
Ascent: 1750'/532m

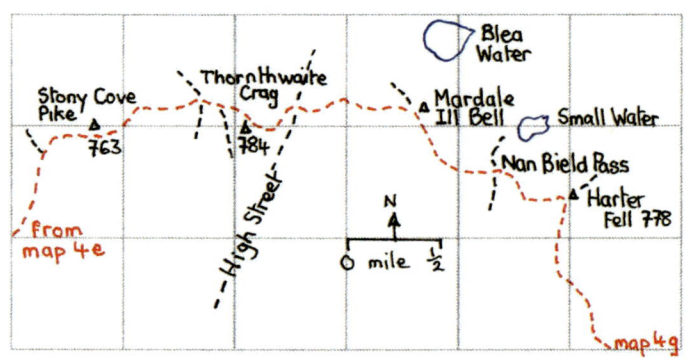

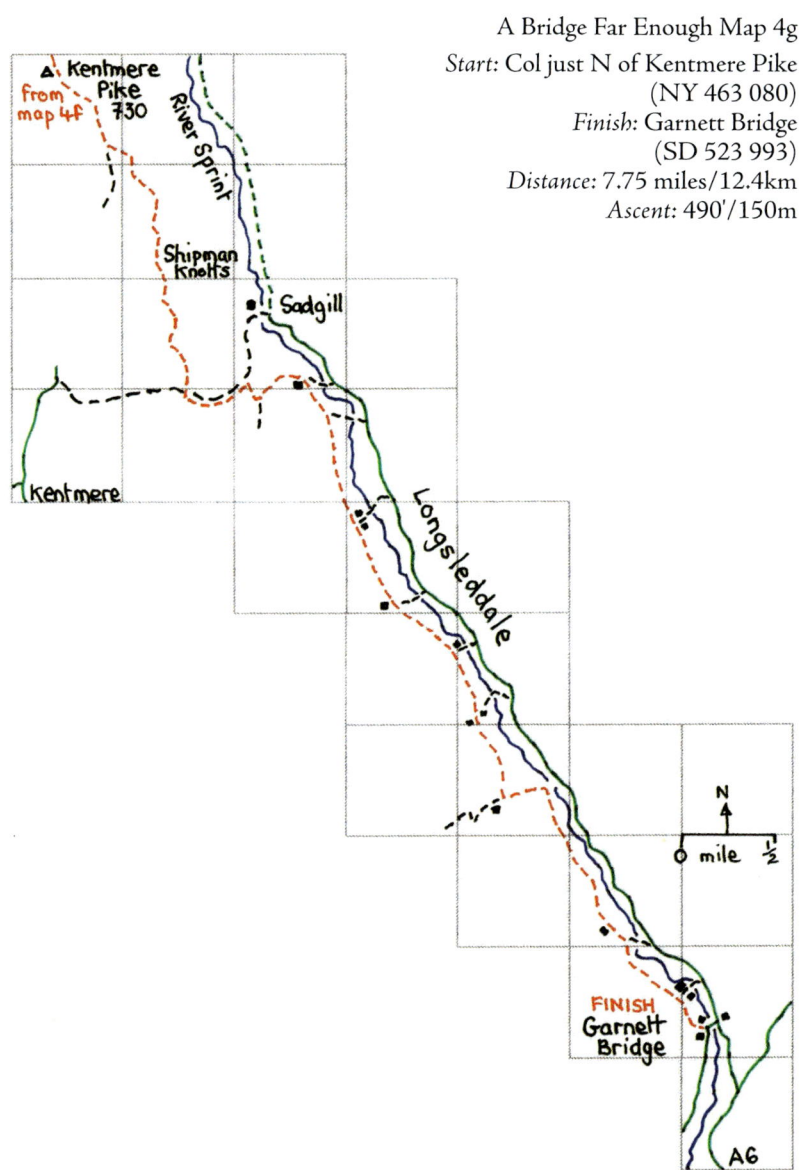

Kentmere
Pike
730

from
map 4f

River Sprint

Shipman
Knotts

Sadgill

Kentmere

Longsleddale

N

0   mile   ½

FINISH
Garnett
Bridge

A6

A Bridge Far Enough Summary

An east/west peak and valley crossing of the Lakes that traces, en route, the District's history and development. A tough mountain challenge with over 13,000' of ascent.

Highest point: Pillar 2926'/892m
Lowest point: Grasmere 230'/70m

5 The Hot Trod

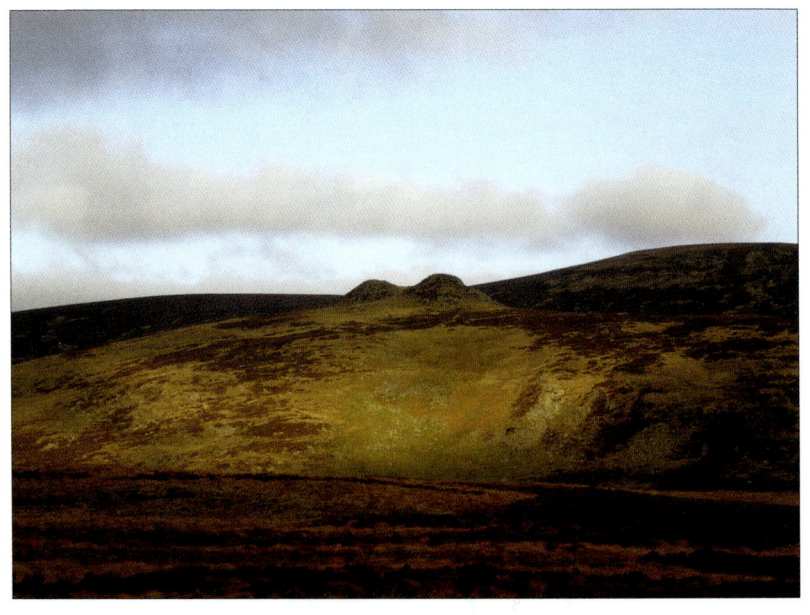

The shapely Great Standrop from High Cantle moor

5 The Hot Trod

Distance: 42.75 miles/68.8km
Ascent: 7950'/2423m
Start & finish: Car-park 1 mile west of Wooler near Brown's Law
(NT 976 272)
Map: OS Explorer 1:25,000 OL16 The Cheviot Hills

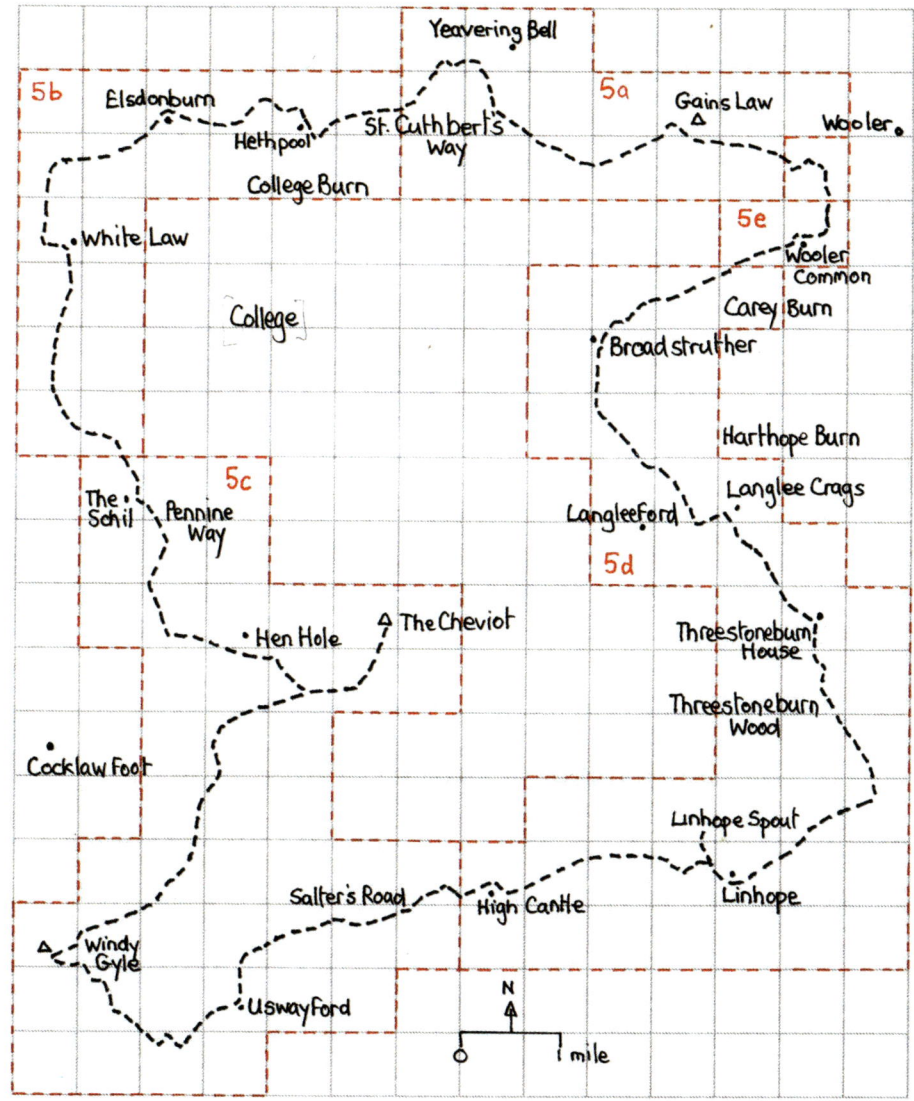

Nearly 1400 years ago and late one afternoon, a young man left the final stretch of remote moorland and, descending a steep wooded hillside, picked up the track that led to the comparative safety of a hamlet by the waters of Wooler. He must have experienced a sense of relief, for he had now passed the rough bounds of a country where careless travellers were likely to disappear without trace and he knew easier going lay ahead. The young man had made good time, for only a few days had passed since his departure from the Abbey at Melrose, charged with a mission that was going to change the course of British history.

The name of the anxious traveller was Cuthbert, whose task was to reach Lindisfarne and persuade King Oswald of Northumbria to forsake the Celtic version of Christianity for that favoured by the Church of Rome, an outcome finally resolved at the Synod of Whitby in 664. Posthumous canonisation inevitably followed. Centuries later, others would tread in his footprints in a rather different spirit of adventure and, when the time came for a need for such things, the opening of an official route was formally announced. At first, our particular Trod reverses the saint's steps by what has become St Cuthbert's Way, and starts from a neat car-park at the foot of the same wood that marked the first sign of sanctuary.

The car-park at Wooler Common has the usual accoutrements—information board, picnic tables, etc—but once out of the wood such trappings of civilisation fall away and an empty moorland spreads before you. As you climb over Gains Law there are fine views down the northern flanks of White Law and Yeavering Bell towards the river Glen. There lies the Border and, if your ambition is to walk in the North of England, this is as far north as it gets. St Cuthbert's Way now drops towards the border and into the hamlet of Hethpool, where it picks up Elsdon Burn.

It was in these parts another Cuthbert, Lord Collingwood of Trafalgar fame, fearing the navy might run out of mature oak to replace ships lost in action, purchased an estate in Cheviot and, with his pockets full of acorns, wandered far and wide scattering the seeds to the wind. Perhaps he hoped, as a man who had not been fully acknowledged for his contribution to the famous victory,

he would at least be hailed as the saviour of the Navy. Of course, it was to no avail. The trees grew all right, examples still flourish in the valley of College Burn, but by the time enough little acorns (3000 per vessel) had grown into mighty oaks, times had changed and the ships of the line were clad in iron. All rather sad really.

Your part in the saint's peregrinations comes to an end when you bump into another pilgrims' progress. The Pennine Way is one of those 'must-do' things that people have on their wish list. In its early days, many started from Edale, usually carrying a plethora of domestic appliances on their backs, but after a rain-lashed crossing of the bogs of Kinder and Bleaklow, slunk home, slung their gear under the sink and substituted 'visit Maldives' in their portfolio of ambitions. Gradually more grew in confidence and eventually all shapes and sizes became sufficiently battle-hardened to dare the final 30-mile push from Byrness to Kirk Yetholm. And there is no doubt that much of their success was due to one man and his distinctive topographical style.

When the publishers asked Alfred Wainwright to produce a book on the Pennine Way, he brought to bear the same meticulous approach he had shown in compiling his *Pictorial Guides to the Lakeland Fells*. He first divided the route into five sections, and then persuaded four like-minded enthusiasts to examine the section nearest to their respective homes. The task was to follow the generally supposed route and pinpoint its exact position on the ground. To this end, AW sent them the relevant maps and requested them, after exhaustive local enquiries, to mark the route with different symbols according to the nature of the terrain. To cover their living and travel expenses, he sent each a cheque, with instructions, if there was anything over, to spend it on riotous living.

It is perhaps appropriate that the paths of Cuthbert and Wainwright should cross at this juncture. Each, in his own way, spread his particular gospel. But, whereas the proselytising by the saint of Lindisfarne was deliberate, Wainwright's, at least in the beginning, was very much accidental. He recorded his early exploration of the Lakeland Fells primarily for his own satisfaction and to create an accurate record which he could look back on in old

age. However, once he had finished what was to be Book One of his pictorial guides, he felt other kindred spirits might find some use for it and tentatively approached a local printer with a view to producing 500 copies.

Despite the lack of professional advice and support, the outcome was unprecedented. Members of the general public, understandably anxious not only about tramping on other people's land but also about the potential perils that might be in store, were quickly reassured by the combination of clear, detailed description and Wainwright's non-patronising style and realised they too could enter this magical world. Distribution had to rely on word of mouth but such was its success that reprint followed reprint, as, on the ground, did thousands of fellow travellers. So it was no surprise when they turned to their mentor when they decided to tackle the Pennine Way.

As a consequence, it all seems pretty obvious nowadays with waymarked signposts, well-worn paths and friendly Park Rangers flapping you on your way. Your section follows this pattern and as long as you stay on tracks or well-maintained paths, then walking in the Cheviot is no more arduous than walking in the Lake District. Indeed there are sections of the Pennine Way that are so paved and mollycoddled that you may as well be promenading along Oxford Street. But beware—once off the beaten track matters change dramatically. In 1938 Mabel Barker who, among other achievements, was the first woman to climb the Central Buttress of Scafell and complete a traverse of the Cuillin Ridge in under 24 hours, decided, with friend and dog, to follow the English/Scottish Border from Berwick on Tweed to the sands of the Solway Firth. Apart from the difficulty of locating the actual boundary and the inconvenience of leaving and rejoining the route to find overnight shelter, the walking itself was often not easy. This was especially true on the traverse of the then pathless Cheviot. As Barker reported in the *Fell & Rock Journal*, peat and heather made for very hard going, particularly when exacerbated by clumps of tussocky grass that break up any attempt to maintain a regular rhythm of movement. In case anyone should be tempted to mutter about the shortcomings of the weaker sex, he might consider

that six years later a group of 28 paratroopers, already toughened up by a fortnight in the Peak, set out to walk in a direct line from Wooler to Edale. During the first 48 hours of this Proto-Pennine Way they had covered a mere twenty miles and more than half of the party had dropped out. The Misses Barker and Short, not to mention Roc the dog, travelled across the same country, covering 25 miles in a single day.

Nowadays it is much easier going as you gain height over The Schil before turning towards the summit of Cheviot itself. You pass a refuge and, as you swing round to your left, you can look down on a jumble of rocks known locally as the Hen Hole. As no self-respecting poultry would dream of making this hovel their abode, there must be some other explanation. One possibility is that it is a corruption of an Old English word meaning evil or hiding place and historically it was a bleak enough spot to act as a rendezvous for ne'r-do-wells or manufacturers of illicit liquor. It was also the supposed bolt-hole of Black Adam who, descending on a nearby wedding, raped and murdered the bride and seized the wedding gifts before fleeing to his lair. The groom, understandably upset, tracked the murderer to the rocky fastness and after suitably bloody battle sliced him to pieces. The mist is starting to gather. Best move on.

Our more peaceful path continues to contour the head of the valley and, above the point where the burn begins its journey towards Cocklawfoot, a decision has to be made. The summit of Muckle Cheviot is on neither our route nor the Pennine Way and if you wish to complete all the County Tops on your travels you will have to make a detour totalling two and a half extra miles. There is still a long way to go but, if you decide to travel that particular extra mile, you will find yourself in an interesting position. Although this is not the Pennines, it feels like the tip of the backbone of England. Here, there is a sharp narrowing as the land is pincered by the North Sea and Irish Channel. It is not much more than 30 miles to the coast in either direction and although there are narrower stretches north of the Highland Line, you can understand why the Romans and their successors decided this was the point to grab Britain by the throat.

Once back on the main line, follow the border as far as Windy Gyle where you abandon the beaten track, turning sharp left for the remote farm of Uswayford (if forced to ask locals the way, try 'Yoozey Ford'). This at one time laid claim to being the remotest B&B in Britain and was used to bisect the last drawn-out gasp of the PW. Although a haven no more, all is not lost. The locals have to be adaptable to survive in these parts and, if required, independent local transport can be arranged to collect and drop travellers at Chew Green, thus subtracting five or so miles and a few hundred feet of ascent from the final long day. Uswayford, meanwhile, is back with the sheep as its only overnight visitors.

Man tends to be generous in its praise of most domestic animals, (the strength of the ox, the fidelity of the hound, etc) but the poor old sheep, whether from political commentators or chanting football mob, tend to get an indifferent press. This scarcely gives them their due. They are relatively cheap to keep as they will eat most things and stay put without elaborate enclosures, and over four centuries the wool trade was the basis of Britain's wealth. Perhaps, most importantly, the especial warmth of their fleece allowed the agrarian society of the Middle East to develop protective clothing to combat the colder climes of Northern Europe. Farming meant food production on a large scale, thus freeing up part of a growing population to specialise in the Arts and Sciences. No sheep—perhaps no Renaissance, no New World, no trips to the Moon.

The next stage of our journey offers easier going. Linhope is reached by following the Salter's Road through the forest until you join a track below the broad ridge of High Cantle. Here there is a choice of a high or low road. The former is the better as, for some reason, constructed tracks seem unending, whereas paths with their contour-driven twists and turns offer a variety of surprise views and unexpected pleasure. There is both a configuration of undulating ground that would have graced Page 3 of any Country Life Gazette and the roar of Linhope Spout in spate to catch the eye. The latter is slightly off route but very worth a visit. Once at Linhope, take the track that leaves the settlement in a north easterly direction and aim for the corner of Threestoneburn Wood.

As has already been mentioned, plantations of timber tend to be on the move and it is unwise to rely unduly on even the latest efforts of the Ordnance Survey. Felling can turn sheltered firebreaks into desolate wastes. Rights of Way can be easily blocked and overgrown. As matters stand, you should aim for the south-east corner of the plantation, then follow the boundary fence northwards until a gate allows access. From there to Threestoneburn House is a bit up to you and your compass, but there is a combination of rides and signposted rights of way that lead to the open air. (The pusillanimous, however, can avoid the whole issue by traversing Hare Hill and retuning to the House on a good track.) Once there, navigation becomes simpler. A good path runs below Langlee Crags to join a track that slopes down to the bridge at Langleeford. Here the Harthope Burn can be crossed.

The Harthope Valley is just the place for a picnic and, as the river bank broadens sufficiently for parking and impromptu games of football, an ideal place for a rendezvous. It also offers a quick and easy way to the top of Cheviot, so is well positioned for an early reconnaissance before any attempt on Le Grand Cirque as a whole. We still have five or so miles to go but the going is easy. Good tracks past Broadstruther, a bridge across Carey Burn, and more, but less capricious, conifers lead speedily to Wooler Common and a reunion with St Cuthbert. It is worth keeping your eyes open on this section, one of the last sanctuaries of the indigenous red squirrel. It may not be too long before its transatlantic cousin takes over, succeeding where other invaders have spectacularly failed.

Readers unfamiliar with this part of the world may well be wondering what lies behind the title of the circuit they have just completed (particularly if their own experience of the walk has been somewhat less than tropical). As already indicated, the border country with its general practice of skullduggery was not the place for faint-hearts. Successive would-be conquerors had tried to impose their rule of law on these parts and, in turn, Romans, Vikings, Normans came, saw and decided they didn't fancy their chances. Eventually the King in London gave up the unequal struggle and, hoping for the best, left the inhabitants to their own

devices. As a result, the process of justice was rough and ready, reminiscent of the gun law of American frontier towns.

One of the remedies for perceived injustice was the proclamation by the March Warden to allow a 'Hot Trod'. This permitted a posse of men to be formed, with the authority to raise 'a hue and cry' and scour the neighbourhood for stolen livestock and the like. It was led by the Warden himself who, as a badge of office, caused an outrider to carry aloft a piece of flaming turf spiked on the point of a spear. Once formed, these vigilantes were, for six full days, legally allowed to roam the district at will, regardless of national or other boundaries. To be woken in the middle of the night by the clatter of fully armed men accompanied by baying hounds must have been a fearsome moment and as we drop into the now peaceful Wooler, we should consider the advantages of living in gentler times.

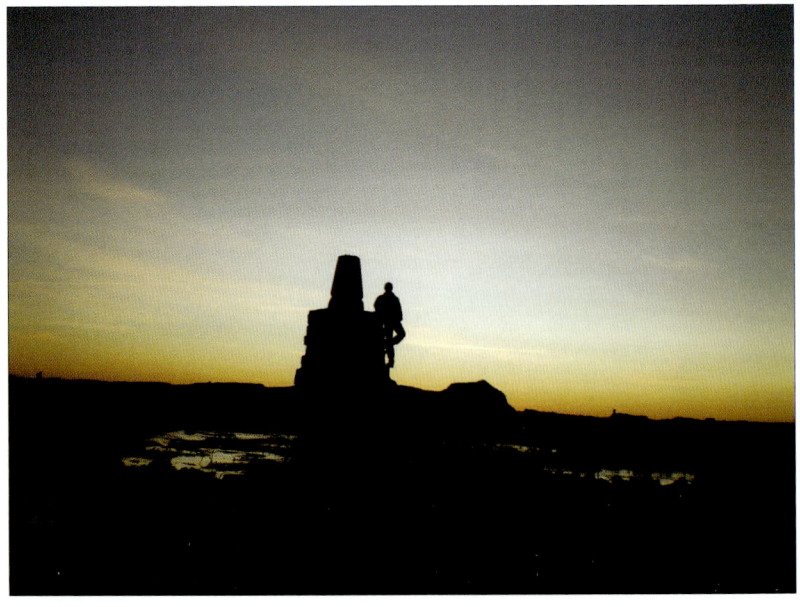

The Cheviot summit at sunset

The Hot Trod Map 5a

Start: Car-park near Brown's Law (NT 976 272)
Finish: Just SW of Torleehouse (NT 910 286)
Distance: 5.5 miles/8.7km
Ascent: 850'/260m

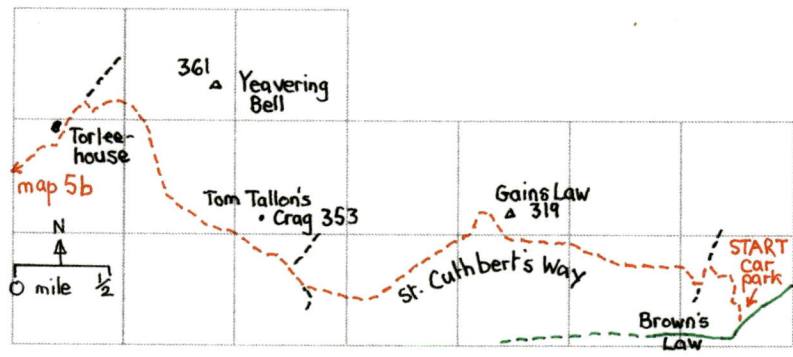

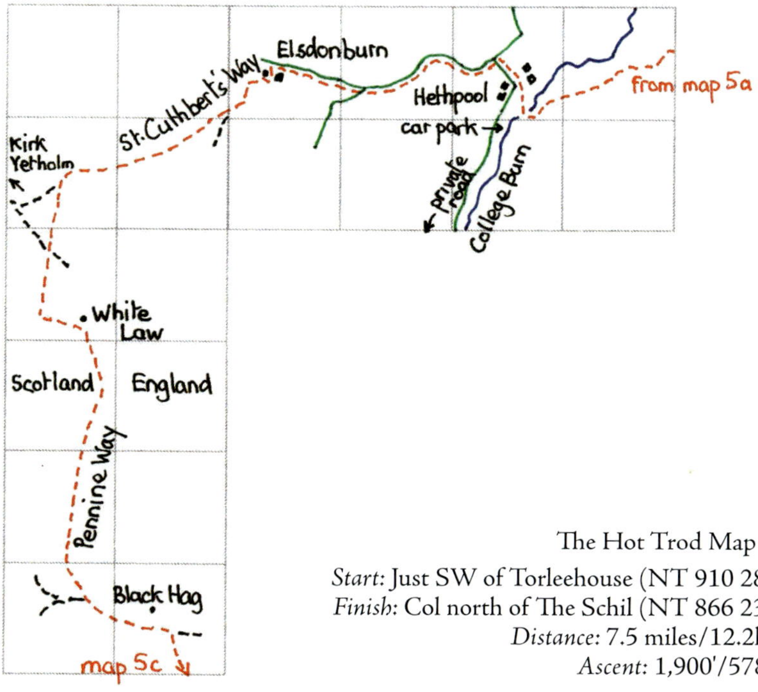

The Hot Trod Map 5b

Start: Just SW of Torleehouse (NT 910 286)
Finish: Col north of The Schil (NT 866 230)
Distance: 7.5 miles/12.2km
Ascent: 1,900'/578m

The Hot Trod Map 5c

Start: Col north of The Schil (NT 865 230)
Finish: Track near High Bleakhope (NT 920 162)
Distance: 15.5 miles/24.9km
Ascent: 2960'/903m

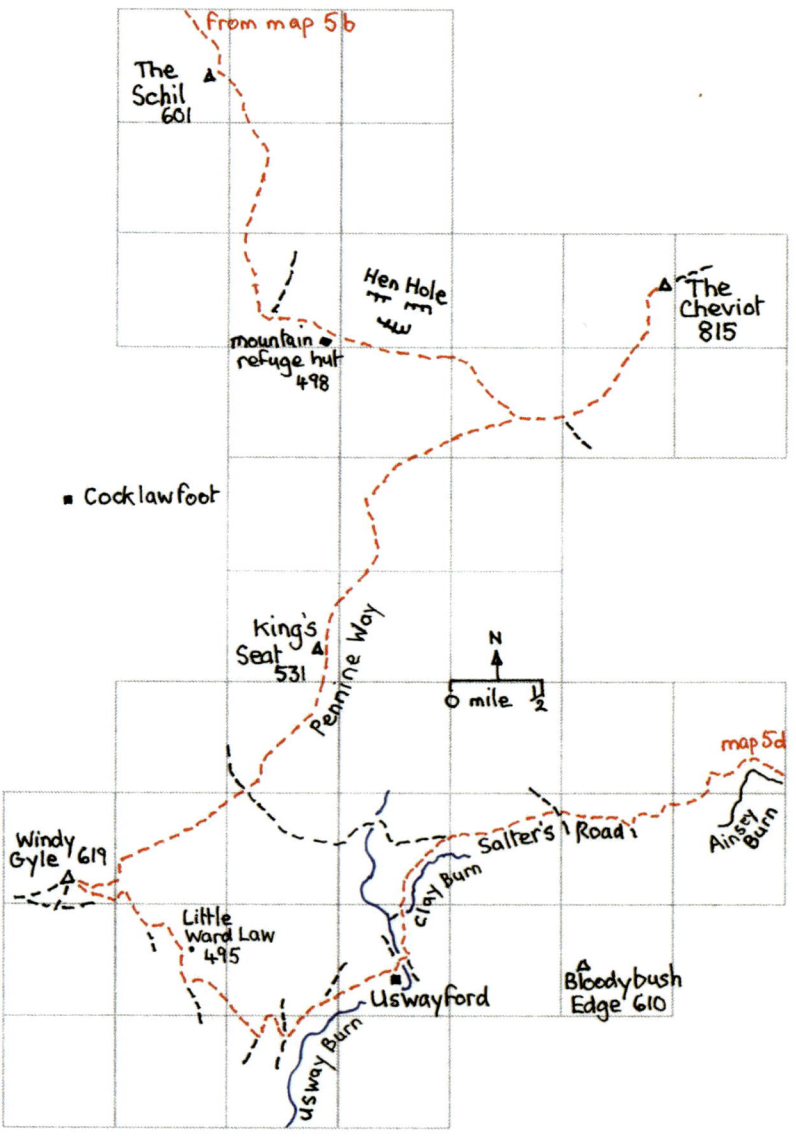

69

The Hot Trod Maps 5d & 5e
Start: Track near High Bleakhope (NT 920 162)
Finish: Car-park near Brown's Law (NT 976 272)
Distance: 14.25 miles/23km
Ascent: 2240'/682m

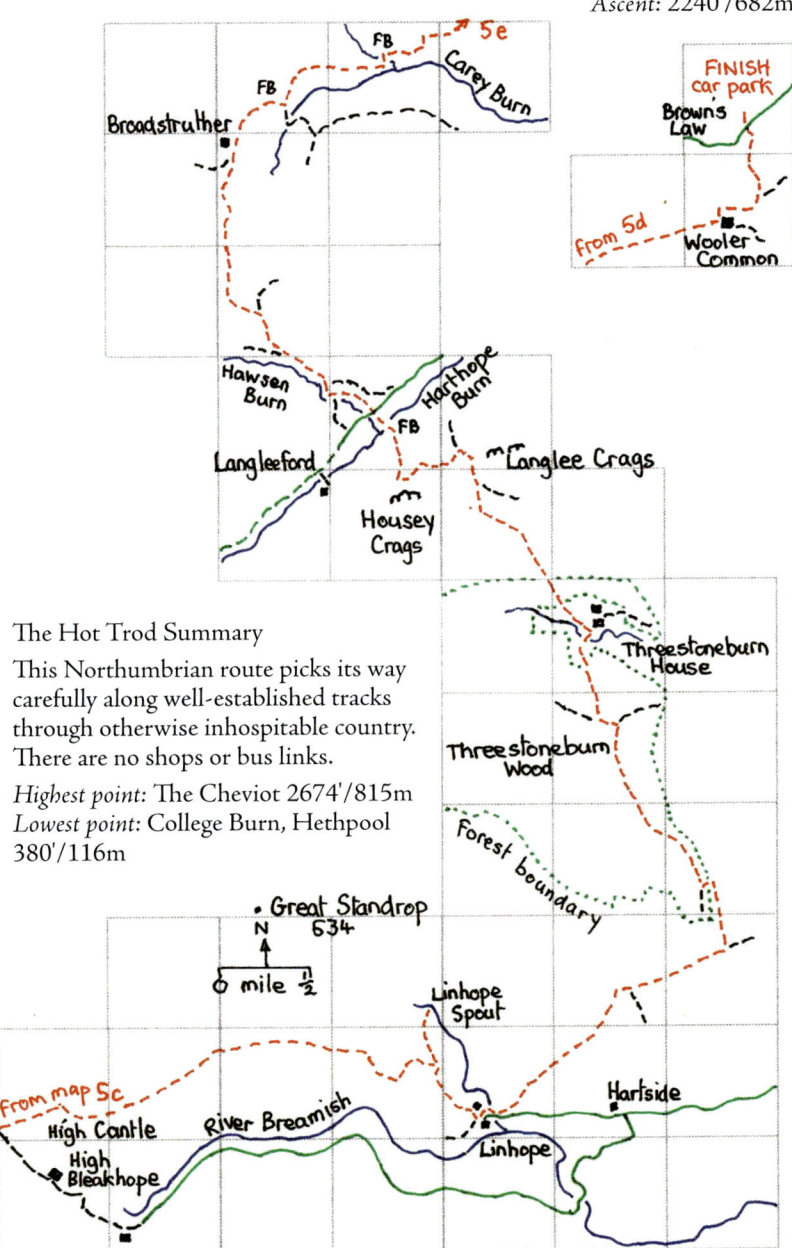

The Hot Trod Summary

This Northumbrian route picks its way carefully along well-established tracks through otherwise inhospitable country. There are no shops or bus links.

Highest point: The Cheviot 2674'/815m
Lowest point: College Burn, Hethpool 380'/116m

6 The Real Pennine Way?

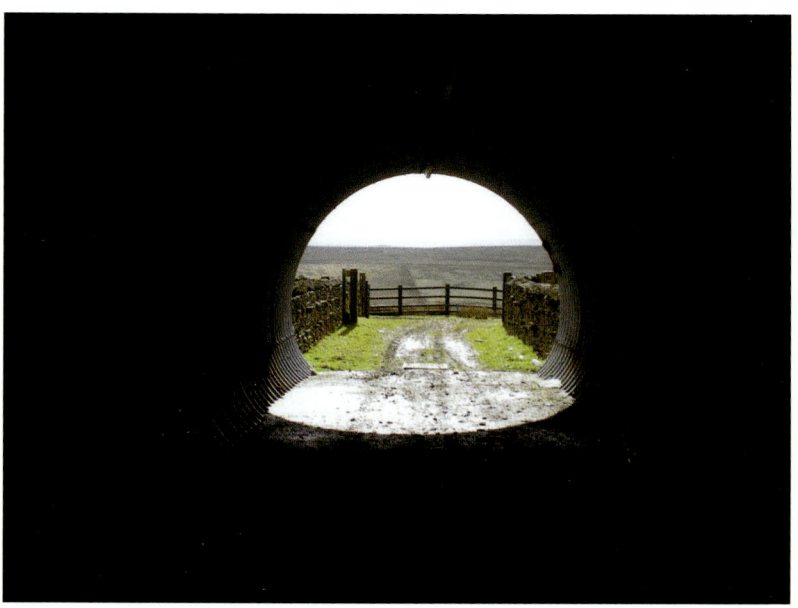

Tunnel under the A66

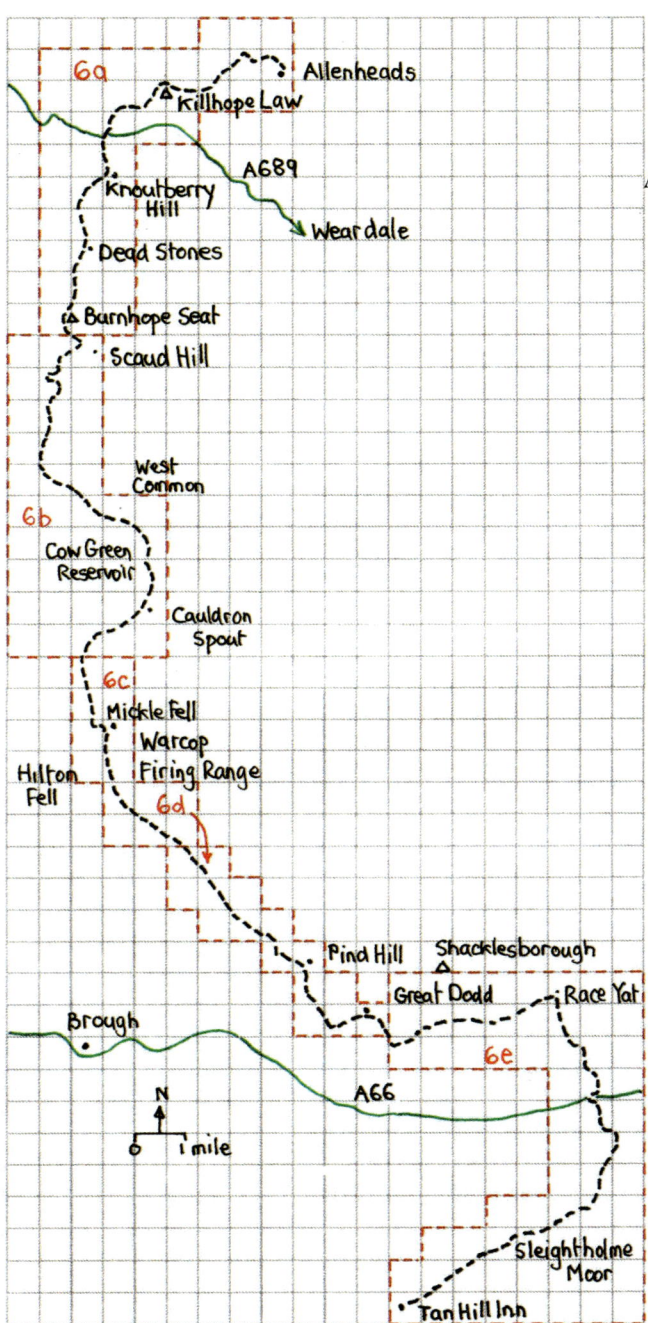

Distance:
42.5 miles/
68.4km
Ascent:
5050'/1540m
Start:
Allenheads Inn
(NY 859 453)
Finish:
Tan Hill Inn
(NY 896 067)
Maps:
OS Explorer
1:25,000
OL16 North
Pennines &
OL19
Howgill Fells

6a

Allenheads

Killhope Law

A689

Knoutberry
Hill

Weardale

Dead Stones

Burnhope Seat

Scaud Hill

West
Common

6b

Cow Green
Reservoir

Cauldron
Spout

6c

Mickle Fell

Warcop
Firing Range

Hilton
Fell

6d

Pind Hill

Shacklesborough

Great Dodd

Race Yat

Brough

6e

N

A66

0   1 mile

Sleightholme
Moor

Tan Hill Inn

In 1965 the Pennine Way was officially opened. For some, it created a test of endurance and determination that offered a good way of working up the necessary sweat to offset a sedentary lifestyle. For others, it was the end of a long struggle for access to land that historically belonged to us all. Yet if the original hopes were for a path to run along the 'Backbone of England', this ambition appears to have been dashed. A conflict of interests was inevitable, with a number of diversions being forced on the planners, and there was no greater swerve than that round the profitable grouse moors lying between the Tan Hill Inn and Killhope Cross. At this point, chastened Pennine Wayites are forced to slope off towards Middleton-in-Teesdale. A pleasant enough diversion and a chance to see some decent waterfalls but thereafter, with the exception of an excursion to the top of Cross Fell, the Way is driven from the higher ground to follow the valley as far as Hadrian's Wall. For those with a glint in their eye, it avoids the main challenge.

The true watershed reflects the historical Durham/Cumbria border and in doing so crosses a County Palatinate where once the powers of the Clergy outweighed those of the King. It travels from the northern borders of Yorkshire to the heights above Allendale and the beginnings of Northumberland. For the most part, our route brooks no obstacle and the country crossed is as rough as you like. It is the sort of terrain where paths never get started and horses disappear without trace. Moreover, there is a strong chance that you may be used as target practice by gung-ho Territorials. It is not for the faint-hearted but, as I have said elsewhere, when the going gets tough, the North gets going.

And it is in the North we begin. Our starting blocks are set in the isolated village of Allenheads. Surprisingly, although we are well south of the Tyne, we are still in Northumberland, but by the time Killhope Law has been passed the route lies firmly (if it can be so described) within the land of the Prince Bishops. Here it stays until at the last it joins the Pennine Way to sneak into Yorkshire and the bar of the Tan Hill Inn. It is a long and at times arduous journey but once ensconced before a blazing fire with a pint of Theakstons to hand, you can gain a deal of satisfaction from knowing you have crossed the whole of a county in one go.

Allenheads is mining country, but not for the usual fossil remains found in a traditional north-east coalfield. The mineral extracted hereabouts is lead and our route starts on the Carriers' Way, which connects the Killhope mine to the local smelt mills. As you would expect, this is a well-constructed track, further improved by the need to carry shooting parties to the higher ground. Even when it is left and you strike up to Killhope Law, the going is easy and good time can be made. But don't be fooled—you are being flattered to be deceived. Once the summit has been left, with its conglomeration of cairn, mast and trig point, matters begin to alter. The point on the road that is your next objective appears near enough to offer no serious problem. And it is near enough—less than two miles away and downhill to boot.

Even the initial descent is straightforward but once the land levels, the outlook deteriorates. There are two problems. First, unless there has been a long dry spell, much of the surface can be so sodden that it forms unfathomable mire and you are forced to detour in a somewhat convoluted manner. Second, and as a result of the first, you tend to lose your sense of direction, with your hearing being the best of the senses as it picks up the distant hum of a surprisingly busy A689. Occasionally you manage to stick your head above ground level to get a glimpse of the target, only to plunge once more into another ditch. The whole affair can best be described as a cross between the Battle of the Somme and a rather clammy maze. One final tip is not to be tempted by the tracks made by quad bikes. The weight distribution of these vehicles has been designed to skim over bogs. The human frame has not.

Later, or sooner with careful planning and a bit of luck, you will reach Killhope Cross, the highest classified road point in England, and you realise why the hum of the traffic has been so helpfully consistent. Over a good weekend a procession of motorcyclists generate their own form of excitement by racing the twists and turns, lifts and falls of the tortuous path formed by the roads in these parts. It all seems rather dangerous, some might say foolhardy. But those who, shaking mud out of their hair, have just emerged from a particularly frustrating crossing from Killhope Law to the road are not really in a position to pontificate on the recreational habits of others.

If that is your lot, you will be relieved to know matters get better. The route is now clearly on the watershed between Durham and Cumbria and the boundary line of walls and fences means you can put the map away and switch into autopilot. In fact, such is the navigational ease, you may find time to consider another state of confusion that exists hereabouts. This is tricky territory for the ticker of lists, particularly if the ticking in question relates to the collecting of County Tops. And the tickers' dilemma has been caused by successive governments fiddling with constituency boundaries in order to safeguard their majority.

On the whole, these gerrymanderers concentrate on areas with an electorally relevant population and, as sheep can't vote, leave mountainous tops alone. But in 1974 there were significant changes. Much to the locals' annoyance, large chunks of Yorkshire went to bed confident in the knowledge of their own identity, only to wake up sporting the red rose, and a large slab of Lancashire found itself in the newly created county of Cumbria. Nor did the mountain tops escape political shuffling. There was a certain logic in Coniston Old Man being returned to the bosom of the Lakeland Fells, but there was less in leaving Lancastrians with a County Top, Gregareth (formerly of Yorkshire), half-way up an even higher hill in Cumbria.

By the time you've got your head round the fact it's nowadays possible to ascend one County Top when going downhill and discover a passenger sitting on the upper deck of a passing omnibus would be higher than another, you have probably decided gathering wool is a more profitable exercise. But, in the positive column, you will have successfully spludged your way over Knoutberry Hill, Nag's Head and Dead Stones to reach the summit of Burnhope Seat, the County Top of the old County Durham. If, however, you are determined to tick off the highest point of any county that is or was, there's a further problem. The summit cairn is, in fact, in Cumbria and the highest point of Durham is a few feet lower, languishing on a somewhat undistinguished bed of mud and stones. The highest summit in Durham, i.e. where the ground falls away in all directions, was, before the reorganisation of 1974, Scaud Hill, lying a little to your east.

Even before reaching the B6277, you have probably had enough of cartographical conundrums and soggy peat, so it is good to find a straightforward miners' track and for the first time since Killhope Law you can concentrate on the view and not on your feet. This leads to the vast expanse of Cow Green Reservoir and, if you're any sort of a botanist, it's worth having a good look around as you go. Much of the flora is unusual and at times unique to this area, as one of the unlikely effects of the toxic waste strewn by lead mining was to encourage some improbable species to flourish.

The 772 square miles that make up this Area of Outstanding Natural Beauty is also the point where the incipient Tees, fed by the likes of Force Burn, begins its voyage to the coast. The whole locality you are passing through is an important gathering ground. For not only the Tees but also the Tyne and Wear start their journey in these parts, creating the waterways that were to combine the towns at their mouths into one of the biggest shipbuilding precincts in the World. The Reservoir road leads to the dam and the top of Cauldron Snout, where the Tees begins a series of impressive sudden drops towards the North Sea and we join with the Pennine Way previously diverted through Middleton. Follow the Way for a short distance to a disused mine before heading south over Mickle Fell and down the other side to the B6276.

Except it's not quite as easy as that. The first obstruction is Maize Beck, a tributary of the Tees which, unlike its parent river, has no volume control in the form of a reservoir dam. After heavy rain it may be impossible to ford and it could look as if you have come to a full stop. The Pennine Way, fortuitously, comes to the rescue, for its pilgrims have also to reach the other side. A bridge has now been constructed and, though not situated for your convenience, lies little more than a mile upstream.

This short zigzag should not delay you for long and it is as nothing when compared to the awaiting hazard. You are now on the edge of the Warcop Firing Range and for much of the year the military deem it necessary to launch exploding missiles into the area. But, as with all wars, there is the occasional truce and walkers can cross unmolested. Details of dates and times are to be found on the website of Warcop Firing Range. This might appear

a rather limiting inconvenience but it is also shell-free on Sunday afternoons so, with a bit of planning and long daylight hours, it is possible to plan your crossing to coincide with the abeyance.

You know you have rejoined the correct line of ascent when you come across a numbered line of boundary stones (counting down from 101) and these can be followed all the way as far as Great Dodd, when the A66 and your final destination are in sight, if not immediate reach. At the watershed between Mickle and Hilton Fells a substantial fence bars your way and forces a detour to the summit plateau. As with Cheviot, the summit of Mickle Fell does not lie on our actual route but, unlike Northumberland's high point, it offers excellent views in most directions. It's well worth the effort and if by now you have been browbeaten into being a ticker of lists, you will need no urging.

Provided there are not spate conditions in Connypot Beck (the easy interchange of 'Beck' and 'Burn' in these parts is as much a topographical marker as the boundary stones), there should be little problem in picking a route fron the summit to the B6276. Indeed, it is true to say that your greater problems are behind you. The boundary stones, albeit irregularly, and wire fencing guide your path up to Pind Hill, the crossing of Balder Beck and Round Hill. At Great Dodd, follow a line of fencing proceeding due east across Crawlaw Rigg to Race Yat, where you join the Pennine Way meander once more.

When I first researched the route, I thought the final section to Race Yat could be as time-consuming as the stretch following Killhope Law. But after half a mile or so, you should notice a higher ridge appearing to the north of the fence. Every effort should be made to gain this high ground as quickly as possible as it offers not only better views (the curiously shaped Shacklesborough is of particular interest) but also remarkably good going. However it is unwise to assume because you have reached the oft-trod track at Race Yat it's plain sailing for the rest of the journey. The path is at times indistinct and, when crossing Sleightholme Moor, Wainwright rightly likened the ground to porridge in dry conditions and oxtail soup in wet. It has its brighter moments, however, when you negotiate the tunnel under the A66 constructed by man

and the bridge over the River Greta engineered by God. No prizes awarded for guessing the better architect.

Eventually, the last short rise is reached and the Tan Hill Inn is within your grasp. You have come across a variety of unusual features on your walk but none more so than this hostelry. For many years it only existed to serve the needs of men mining for lead in the district and although it can now be reached by car, it still retains that sense of isolation and self-sufficiency I associate with remote island life. On my last visit, a sash window was flung up and a voice wondered whether I would take the dog for a walk. There followed a daily work-out for Lizzie and, as it turned out, for most of the local grouse. In many ways the image of one man and his dog seemed to symbolise both the loneliness of the journey and the comparative pleasure of company. Or, to put it another way—if you are not happy with the landlord's choice of bitter, it's a long way to go for the next pint.

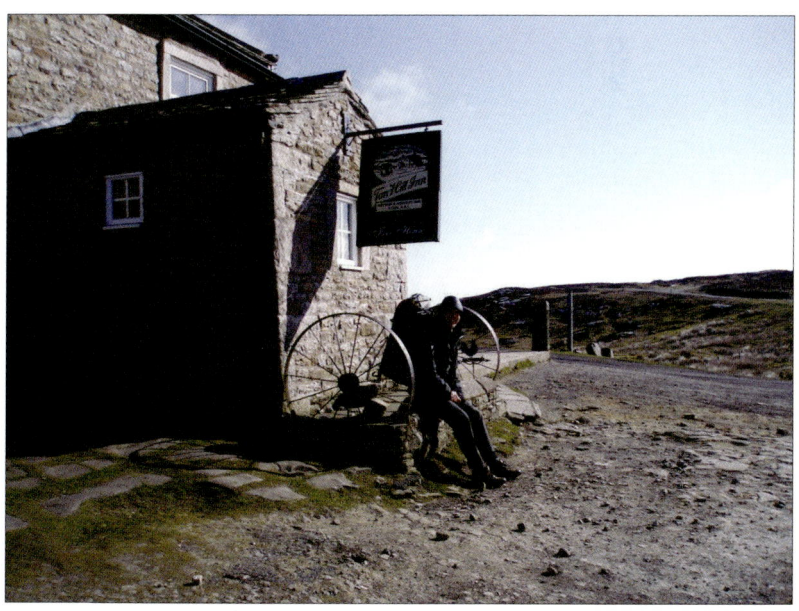

A welcome finishing point

The Real Pennine Way? Map 6a

Start: Allenheads Inn (NY 859 453)
Finish: Just S of Burnhope Seat (NY 789 370)
Distance: 10 miles/16km
Ascent: 1580'/482m

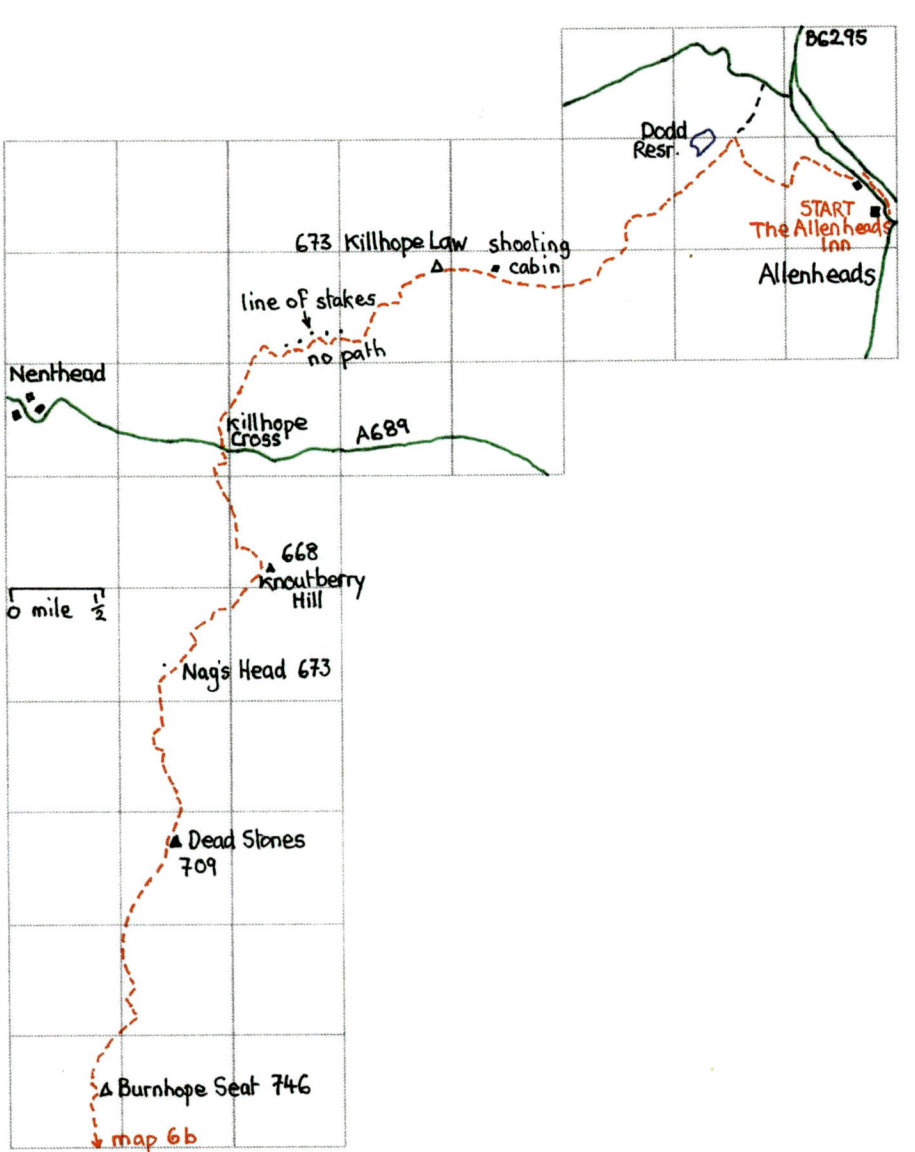

The Real Pennine Way? Map 6b
Start: Just S of Burnhope Seat (NY 789 370)
Finish: Near Maizebeck Force (NY 795 270)
Distance: 9.25 miles/14.7km
Ascent: 590'/180m

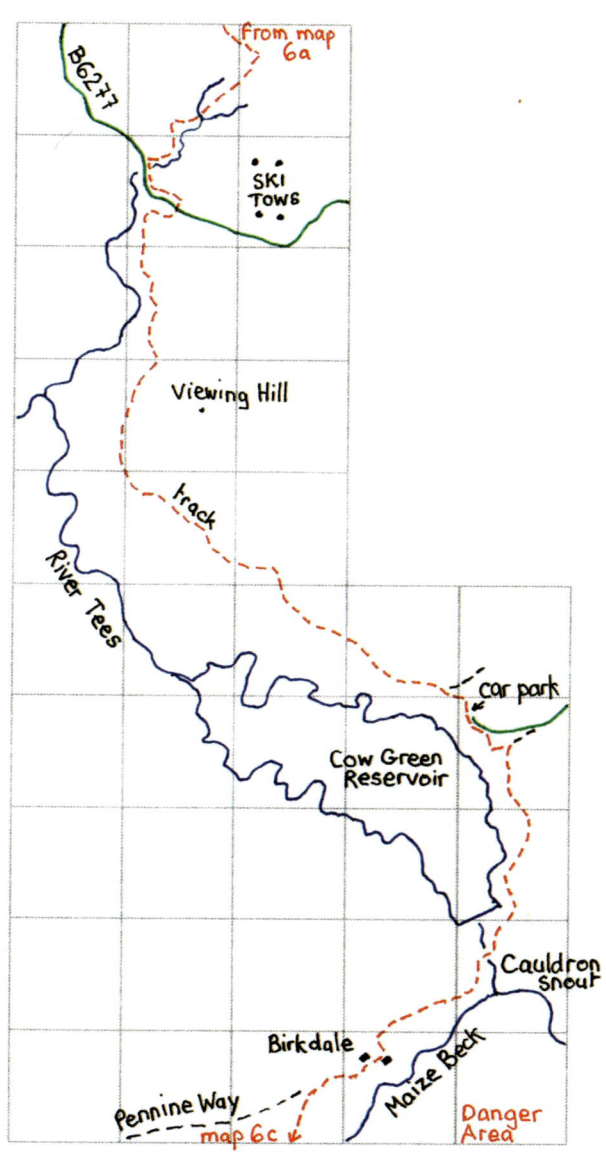

The Real Pennine Way? Map 6c

Start: Near Maizebeck Force
(NY 795 270)
Finish: Hewits
(NY 822 210)
Distance:
4.75 miles/7.5km
Ascent: 1020'/310m

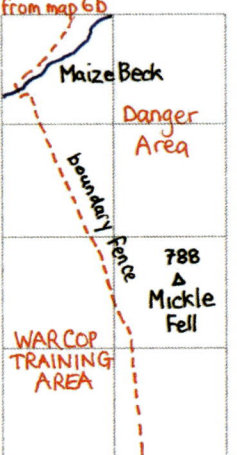

from map 6b

Maize Beck

Danger
Area

boundary fence

788
▲
Mickle
Fell

WARCOP
TRAINING
AREA

Warcop Training
Area is one of
the largest Army
training areas
. in the UK.
Access to this
DANGER AREA
is severely
restricted. Check
www.cumbria.gov.uk
for current details.

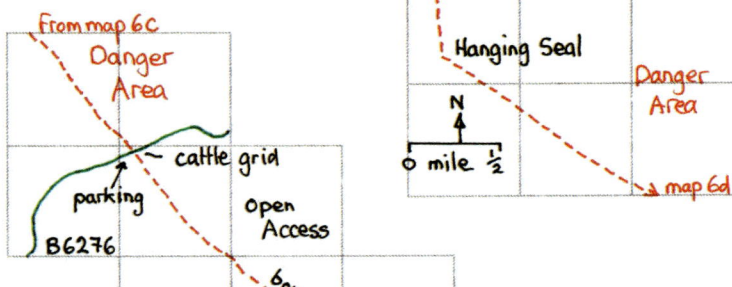

From map 6c
Danger
Area

cattle grid

parking

B6276

Open
Access

Hanging Seal

N
↑

0 mile ½

Danger
Area

map 6d

boundary fence

Pind
Hill

Balder Beck

The Real Pennine Way? Map 6d

Start: Hewits (NY 822 210)
Finish: Just SE of Great Dodd
(NY 890 150)
Distance: 6.25 miles/10km
Ascent: 670'/205m

Great Dodd
471

map 6e

The Real Pennine Way? Map 6e
Start: Just SE of Great Dodd (NY 890 150) *Finish:* Tan Hill Inn (NY 896 067)
Distance: 12.5 miles/20.2km *Ascent:* 1,190'/363m

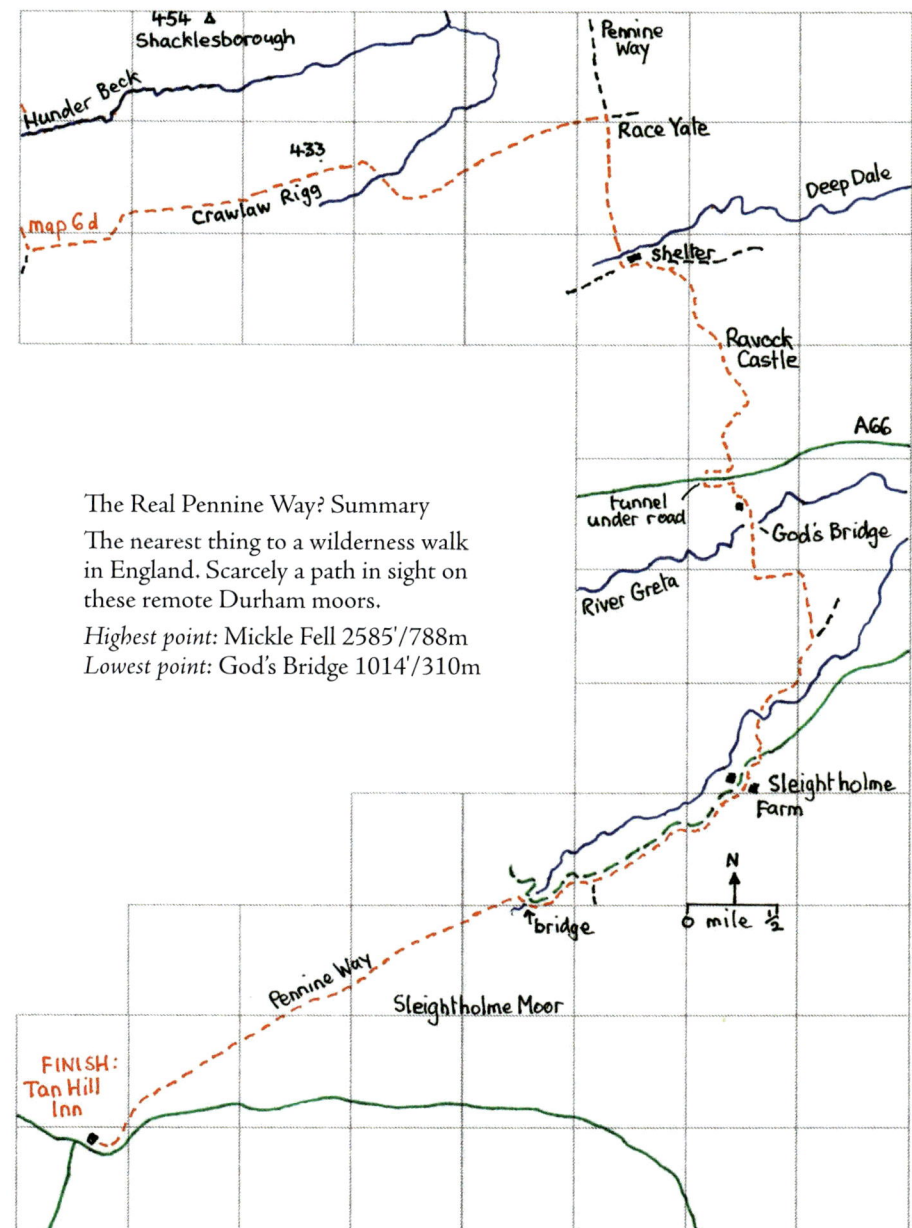

The Real Pennine Way? Summary

The nearest thing to a wilderness walk in England. Scarcely a path in sight on these remote Durham moors.

Highest point: Mickle Fell 2585'/788m
Lowest point: God's Bridge 1014'/310m

7 The Three Peaks and One or Two Others

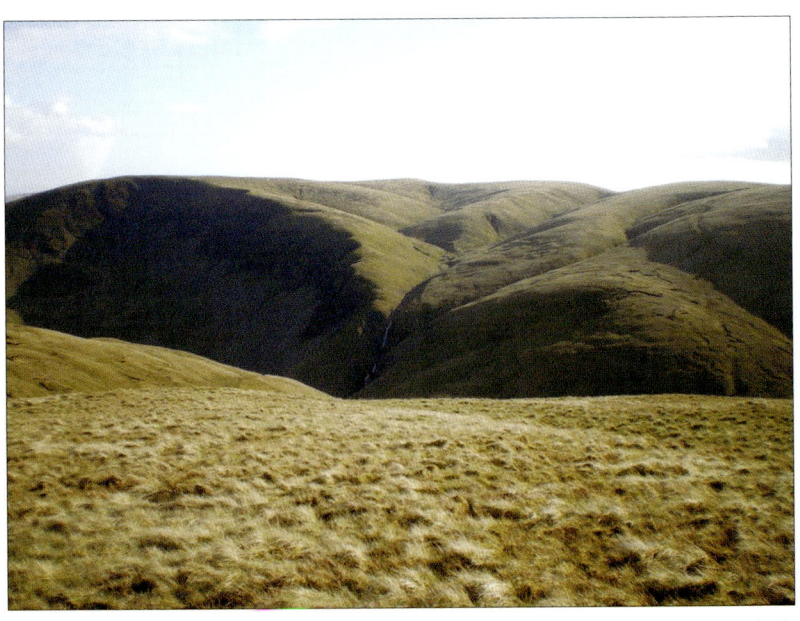

Approaching Cautley Spout from Yarlside

7 The Three Peaks and One or Two Others

Distance: 47 miles/75.5km
Ascent: 12,000'/3658m
Start: Ravenstonedale (NY 722 040)
Finish: Kettlewell (SD 957 722)
Maps: OS Explorer 1:25,000 OL19 Howgill Fells,
OL2 Yorkshire Dales S&W, OL30 Yorkshire Dales N&C

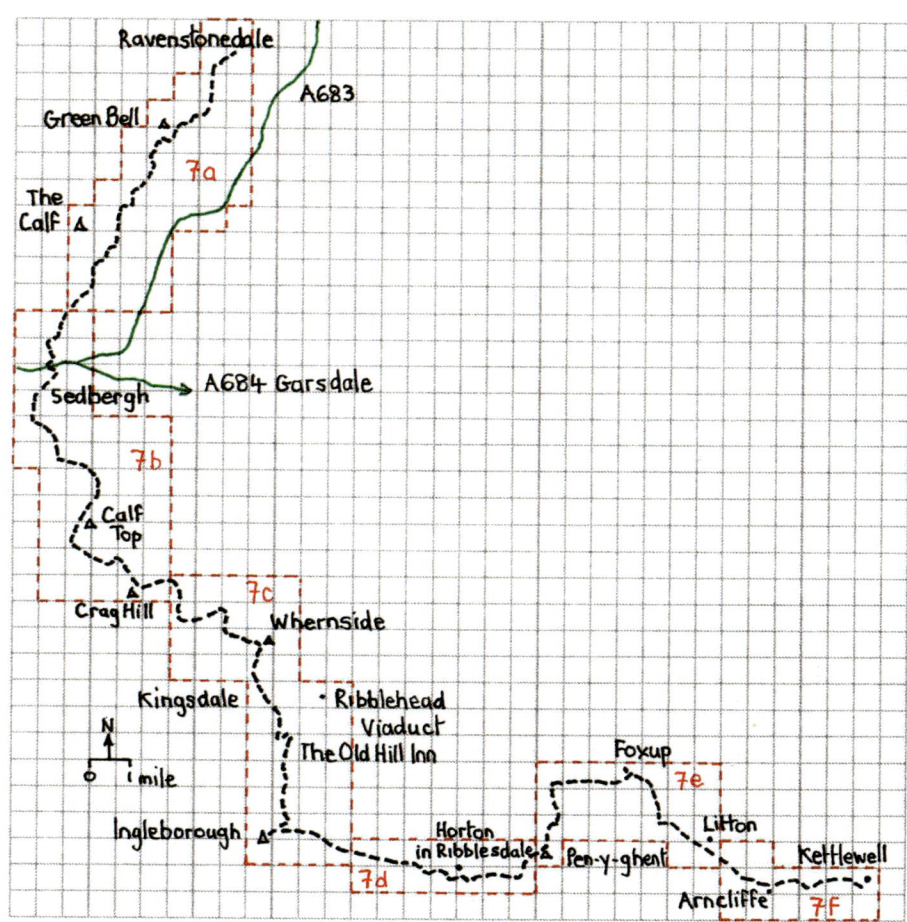

We start at Ravenstonedale, or Rizundal as the locals would have it, and Ravenstonedale is a peculiar place. That is not to say either the village or its local population is in any way eccentric, but that the place itself is a Peculiar. Connoisseurs of the beverages brewed by Theakstons of Masham will be familiar with the term, as Old Peculier is one of the stronger beers this family firm has on offer. Such imbibers could be forgiven for assuming the name is a warning of their possible condition the morning after but they would be wrong. Masham also is, or at least was, a Peculiar, that is to say a defined area which had its own laws and the jurisdiction to enforce them. Among the acts which were considered sufficiently flagrant to require a hefty fine were playing football, marrying outside the parish and, peculiarly to Ravenstonedale, eavesdropping.

The village is also interestingly placed. It lies roughly half-way between the Far Eastern Fells of the Lake District and the line followed by the hordes that tramp between Edale and Kirk Yetholm. Wainwright's Coast to Coast runs across its bows a mile or so north and those twin arteries of commerce and recreation, the M6 and the Settle to Carlisle railway, whistle past at a reachable distance. In many ways this should be the epicentre of hill walking in the Northern Pennines, but many of the fells seem sadly neglected.

At least, this is my experience. I have visited the likes of Great Coum and Wild Boar Fell on more than a dozen occasions and have rarely seen a soul with or without his proverbial dog. Even the Howgills, which have been the recipients of a full Wainwright makeover, are not particularly crowded. Perhaps, paradoxically, the Great Man was in part responsible. His recorded opinion that these fells, though delightful in themselves, are a softer alternative to his more rugged Lakeland hills may have persuaded walkers to save their charms for later life. The problem with such pre-geriatric judgment is when eventually you feel the time is ripe, all too often the rot has set in.

But there may be another reason for the general neglect. Although the Yorkshire Dales are among the most tourist-laden parts of Britain, their main attraction to the general public seems to lie with the riverside walks and often spectacular cataracts and waterfalls. In short, an ideal location for family outings

accompanied by picnics or lengthy lunchtime sojourns in the nearby hostelry. So, for most people, the surrounding hills, with the exception of The Three Peaks (of which more later) tend to act more as a backdrop than a physical challenge. My aim was to pick a path through the madding crowd and construct a route that offered the greatest opportunity for peace and solitude. Although you will bump into pockets of civilisation and packs of sponsored walkers, you should be able to wander as lonely as any cloud that might waft across from daffodil land.

Although the proposed route bypasses Sedbergh, I am not suggesting the place should be dismissed and it is well worth a visit on some other occasion. Once in Yorkshire, now in Cumbria, Sedbergh is a happy mix of market town and Lakeland village. It has about it a sense of contented permanence, yet also an air of hustle and bustle. Partly this may be due to its attempt to turn itself into a Hay-on-Wye in the north of England and partly, at least in term-time, to the presence of pupils of Sedbergh School which has long established itself as a centre of athletic excellence.

One of that establishment's achievements is of particular interest to us as the school could be regarded as the birthplace of competitive fell-running. In 1882 the ten-mile dash round the local hills was inaugurated and soon became an annual event in which the whole school took part. In 1913 it was renamed The Wilson Run after an enthusiastic member of staff who injected new life and a national interest into the event. The race continued annually without a break, except for the desperate winter of 1947 and outbreaks of foot and mouth. A record time of 1. 10. 16 was set in 1899 and not surpassed for over three-quarters of a century. You might like to consider the implications of covering ten miles in 70 minutes as you pass over similar ground.

A study of this background material is all very well, but our present route needs to get on with the job by crossing a bridge at the south end of Ravenstonedale and following Wyegarthdale into what appears ever more unfrequented country. First a track, then a path climbs up to Green Bell and the splendidly named Randygill Top before pushing on, first over Kensgriff and Yarlside, to the fine lookout point of The Calf. The main drag now drops to Sedbergh,

but if you wish to avoid the crowds you can veer west-sou-west towards Lockbank Farm. In front of us is proper North Country walking, loftily tracing the line of the dales, until dips in the land allow the ever-steepening valleys to merge with the skyline. Only then, with a skateboarder's swoop, do you rush to meet them, before climbing once more to traverse the length of your next rampart.

Railway companies had to face a similar problem. All their lines in these parts run south/north while, for the most part, the dales rise in the Pennines, then seek outlets to east and west. Engineers did their utmost to keep to the contours but inevitably they came to a point when bridging a valley (thus avoiding the 'swoop') was easier than hacking out the alternative detour. Ribblehead Viaduct is a good example of the lengths to which they were forced to go. The construction is impressive enough in its design but that is only half the story. The weather can be wild in these parts but the odd storm would not have deterred the Victorian paymasters in pursuit of a quick profit. For the workers it must, at times, have been appalling and there is a tale, no doubt apocryphal, but nevertheless emblematic, of a gale blowing with such swirling force that it hurled a workman off one side of the bridge, then, like some child's kite, whisked him under an adjacent arch to land him back on his feet on the other.

But we are again getting ahead of ourselves. There are a good many miles to cover before we get our first glimpse of that spectacular array of arches. From Lockbank, a close study of the OS map shows it is possible to follow rights of way that slip past the outskirts of Sedbergh, cross the golf course and River Dee before climbing back on the roller-coaster some 500 feet below the summit of Holme Knot. You can now begin to tick off the heights that follow the western boundary of the Yorkshire Dales National Park over an S-shape of fells. The mid-point of the S is split by Barbondale, where it is advisable to pick out your road crossing-point while you have a clear view, and each of the curves is peaked by Calf Top and Crag Hill respectively. The chicane once completed, we slide off its tail a little before Green Hill to land on the north end of Kingsdale.

Kingsdale is a bit of a surprise. A hidden valley, it runs north

from Ingleton to the headland of White Shaw Moss. A narrow road works its way up the side of the dale, keeping close to the River Twiss, the waters of which, after collecting the becks of Whernside and Gregareth, plunge over Thornton Force and Pecca Falls into the relative calm of the River Greta. The valley climbs from an altitude of 500 feet, first gradually, then with a sudden leap to reach three times that height before making an abrupt descent into the cobbled streets of the village of Dent. Not for nothing is the head of the valley known as 'Little Switzerland'. In winter, it can be a wild place and more than one car has been involved in a slithering scrabble that ends up in a snowdrift. Our route crosses the road at its highest point and follows a path up a desolate and little frequented flank of Whernside, the first of the Yorkshire Three Peaks. It is likely you will have the place to yourself, accompanied only by the plaintive cry of the curlew or the admonitory 'get back, get back' of a startled red grouse.

Suddenly this all ends. Particularly at a weekend or summer Bank Holiday. For you now have gatecrashed The Three Peaks Circuit and, as if by some black hole, may well find yourself sucked into the flow. The choice of the word 'circuit' was deliberate as the round is not only a continuous loop but also one of Britain's most popular challenge walks. At 25 miles it is about the right length for a charity event and, in addition to the annual fell run, various philanthropists jog, walk or are pushed round in perambulators to raise money for a variety of causes. The odd participant falls down Hull Pot but still they come, waving banners, jangling collection tins and reducing the bar of the Hill Inn to gridlock. I applaud their motives but would rather they chose a less fragile venue.

The easiest way is to go with the flow, but even that is not as straightforward as it sounds. At Horton-in-Ribblesdale, you collide with the Pennine Way and until you reach the top of the third and final Peak you have the additional hazard of dodging and weaving the oncoming hordes who started at Edale. It may be of some help in such times of stress, or when gathered up in the press and returned in triumph to Horton, to recall the observation of Agatha in T S Eliot's *Family Reunion* that travelling in the opposite direction to the madding crowd is not necessarily a mistake.

On reflection, I feel the preceding paragraphs have been less than fair to this particular upland triptych. Whernside, Ingleborough and Pen-y-ghent are arguably individually and certainly collectively the finest English hills outside the Lake District. Each has its contrasting shape and form and, consequently, an ever-changing landscape underlined by the shift between grit and limestone. If you stray a little from the obvious ways, there are enchanting views down the sequestered cul-de-sacs that stretch up from the main dales and a sense of place and history is captured in such names as Quaking Pot and Boggarts Roaring Holes. If this spectacular collection of lumps and bumps had been located in some distant corner of Britain, allowing the flora and fauna to flourish, it would have been regarded as a hidden gem, discussed, over hushed pints, by hardened explorers.

Nevertheless, it is probably best to shuffle swiftly through Horton, climb the third Peak and, after a final look round, dispatch Pen-y-ghent into your rear view mirror. Once Plover Hill is reached, a path takes you down to Foxup and the intriguing hamlets of Littondale. This particular dead-end has escaped the main thoroughfare and there is little doubt that it has always been seen as a bolthole. There is evidence of Bronze and Iron Age settlements that are over 5000 years old and distinct signs of Saxon agricultural practice. Today's seekers after solitude can slip out of an often teeming Wharfedale, confident, even though the dale was the original television location for Emmerdale Farm, that they will not trip over too many tourists bearing a telephoto lens.

As with all remote places, the dale has its own areas of special interest and Litton was once a renowned centre for cock fighting and badger baiting and the name of Arncliffe translates as eagle cliff, which more than hints at the struggle of shepherds trying to safeguard their flock. I remember staying nearby and having to breakfast somewhat uncomfortably under the baleful eye of 'The last Eagle to be shot in The Dales'. But if you want to get the feel of how the place operated centuries ago, you need do no more than visit the Falcon Inn, where no spirits are allowed and the beer is served straight from the barrel in stone jugs to customers sitting at simple wooden tables.

If even this seems overexciting, you can quickly climb out of the dale through Byre Bank Wood before finally crossing Old Cote Little Moor to descend upon Kettlewell. Here you will find a regular, if not frequent, bus service and a variety of opportunities to feed the inner man. It was my original intention to call this chapter 'Out to Grass', with the route finishing at Grassington, thus covering one of the best five miles of The Dales Way, which at this point unexpectedly follows a high-level line of rocky terraces. This elevation gives fine views of the length of Wharfedale and an assortment of limestone curiosities such as Kilnsey Crag and the Conistone Pie. Others, however, put their foot down (or should I say 'feet up'?) and declared enough was enough and I had to concede that my only reason for concocting such a title (and the additional distance) was that it neatly reflected the probable outcome for my floundering hip joints. I had also to accept that it is somewhat easier to cover the ground on the page than it is, shall we say, in a more pedestrian manner.

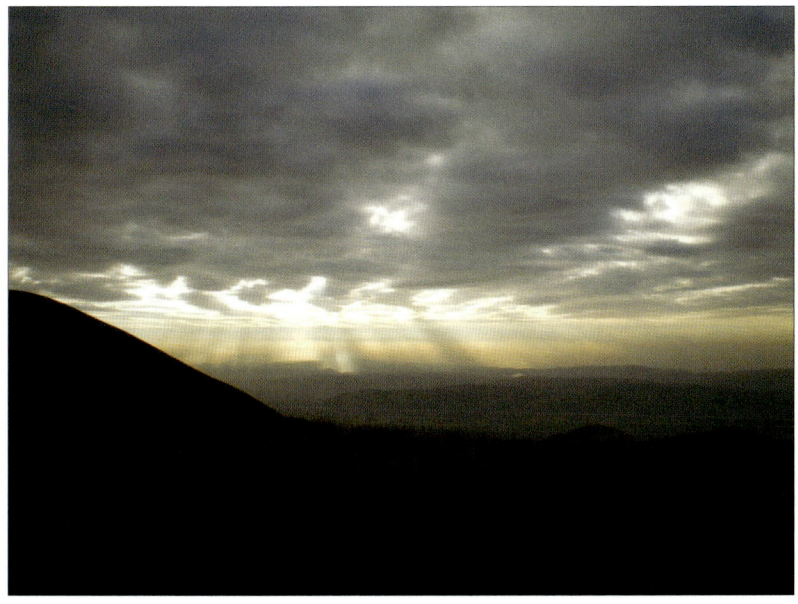

Crepuscular rays from high on the Howgills

The Three Peaks &… Map 7a

Start: Ravenstonedale (NY 722 040)
Finish: Just S of Arant Haw (SD 660 940)
Distance: 8.75 miles/13.9km
Ascent: 3035'/925m

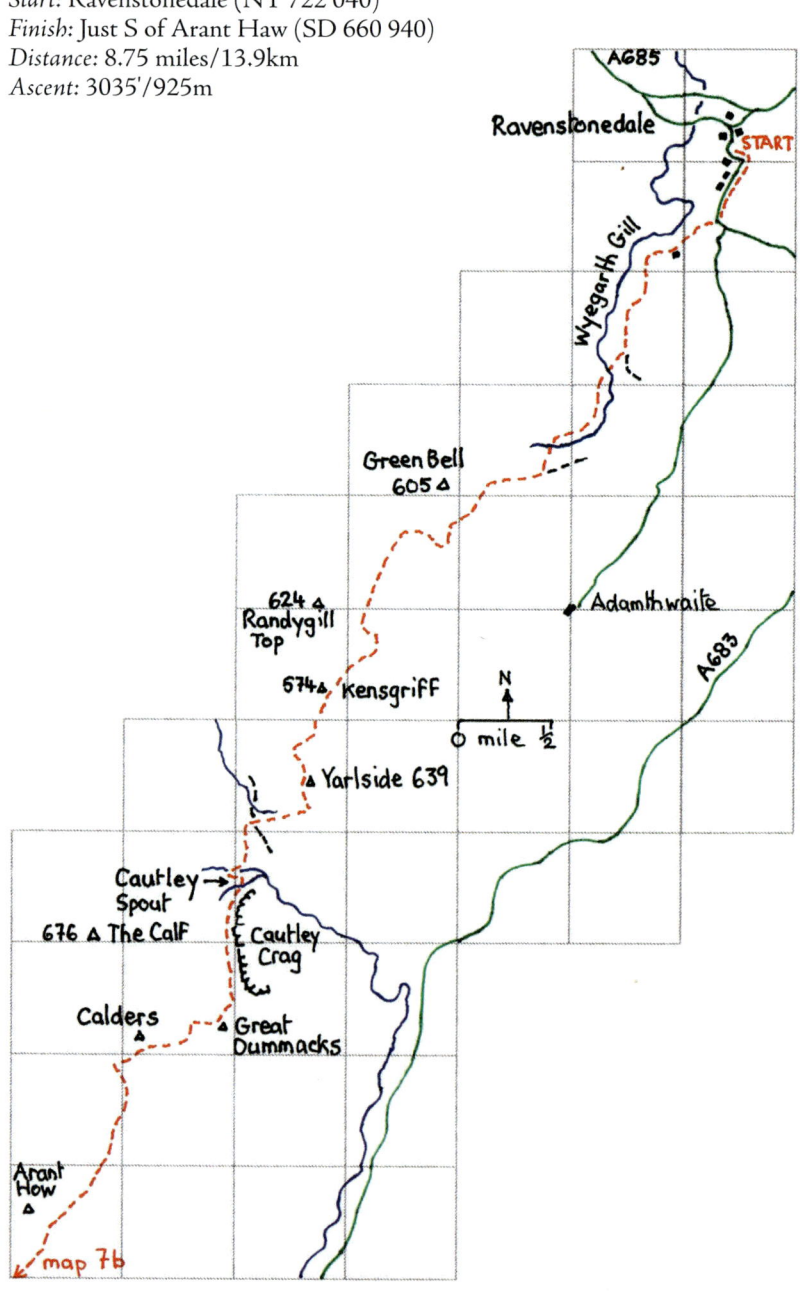

From map 7a

Winder △

Lockbank Farm

supermarket

Sedbergh A683

A684

A683

R. Rawthey

golf course

350 △
Holme Knott

River Dee

Brown Knott

Green Maws

Gawthrop

N

0 mile ½

Calf Top △ 609

very steep

cattle grid

Barbondale

map 7c

Crag Hill △ 682

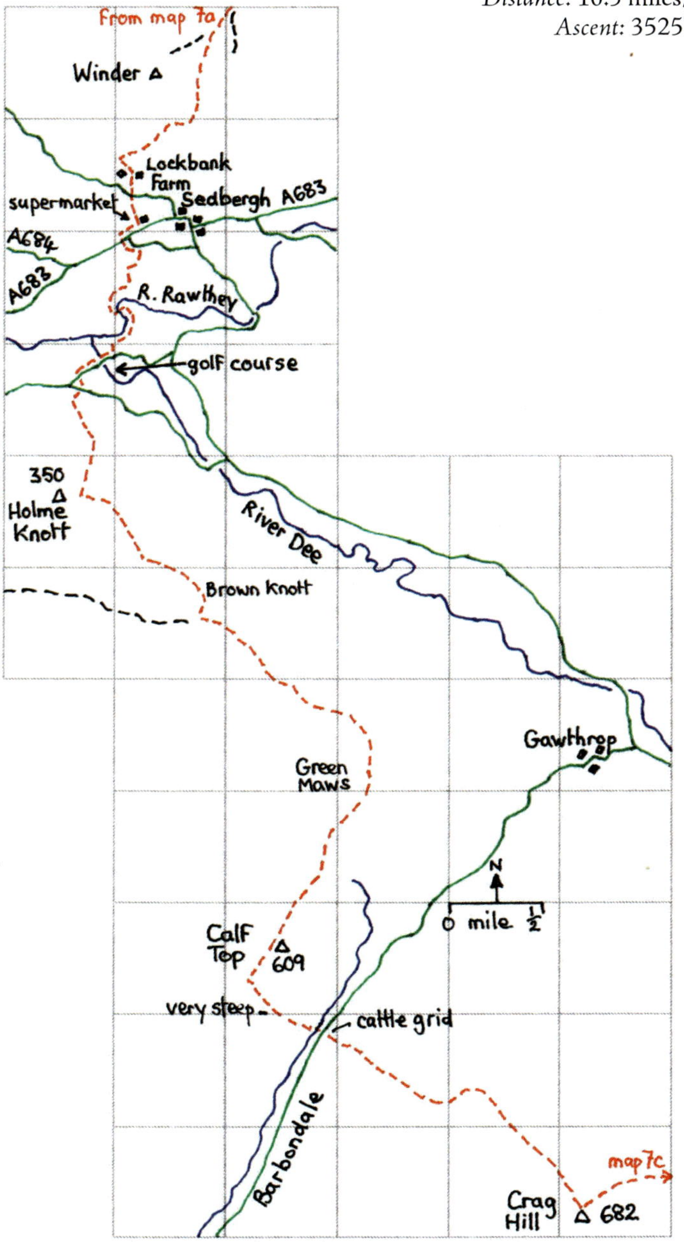

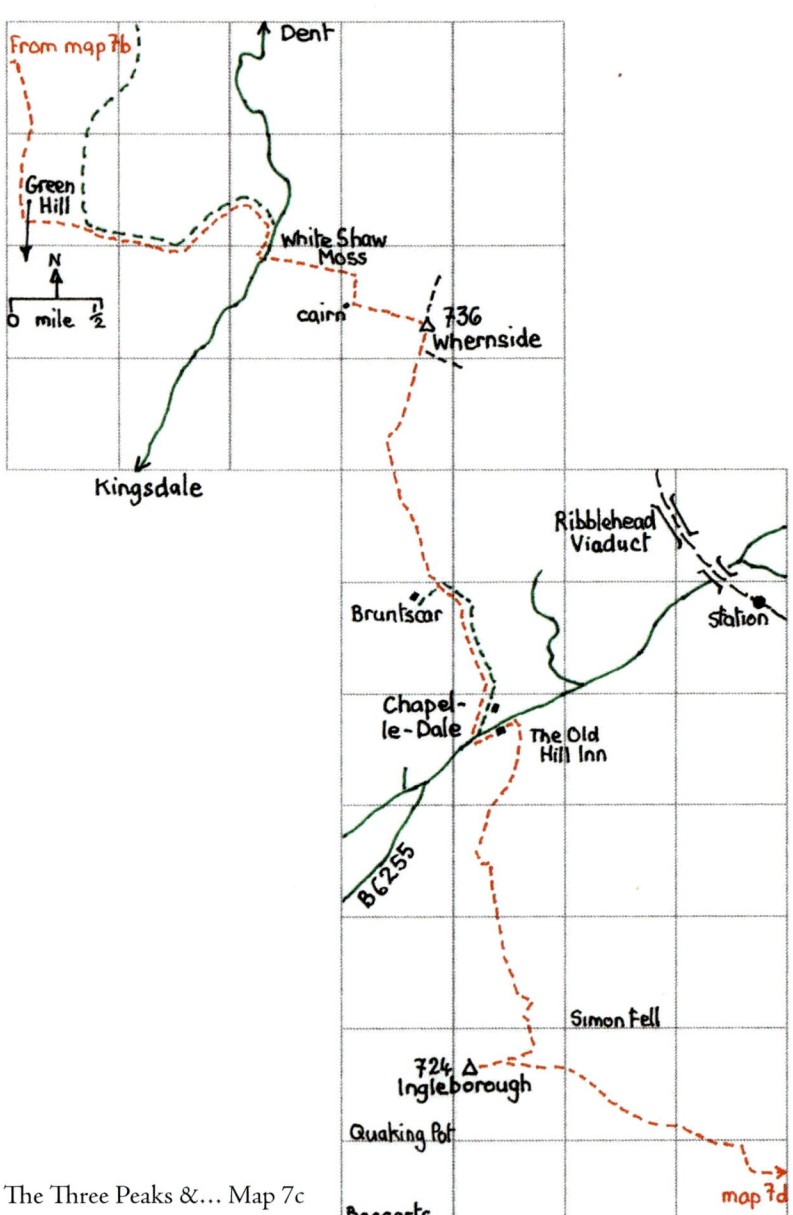

From map 7b

Dent

Green Hill

N

0 mile ½

White Shaw Moss

cairn

△ 736
Whernside

Kingsdale

Ribblehead Viaduct

Bruntscar

Station

Chapel-le-Dale

The Old Hill Inn

B6255

Simon Fell

724 △
Ingleborough

Quaking Pot

The Three Peaks &... Map 7c

Start: Great Coum
(SD 700 835)
Finish: Nick Pot
(SD 770 736)
Distance: 11 miles/17.7km
Ascent: 2580'/786m

Boggarts
Roaring Holes

map 7d

The Three Peaks &… Maps 7d–7f
Start: Nick Pot (SD 770 736); *Finish:* Kettlewell (SD 957 722)
Distance: 16.75 miles/27km
Ascent: 2860'/872m

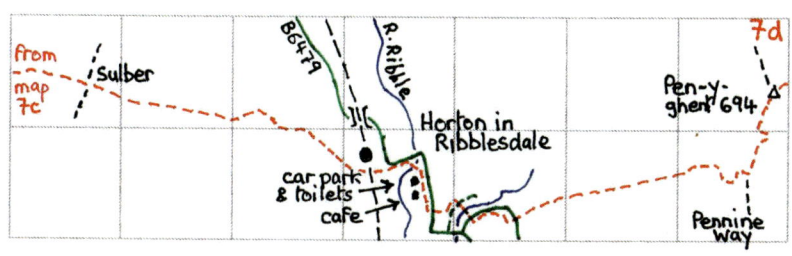

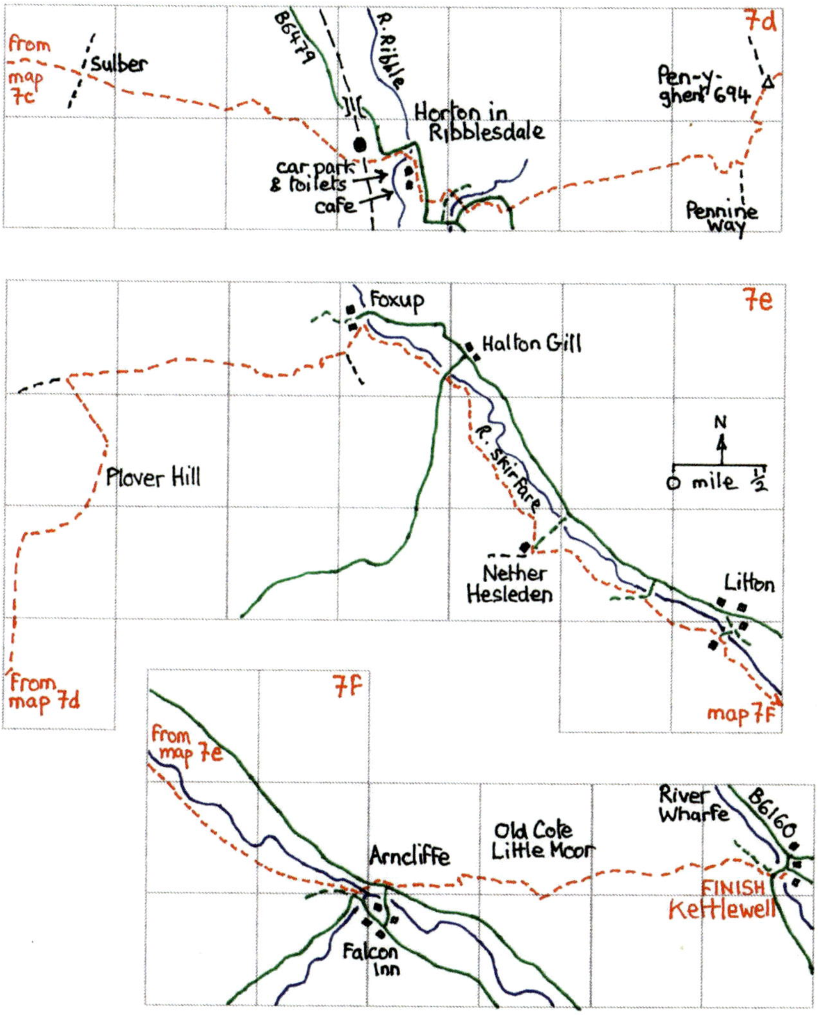

The Three Peaks & One or Two Others Summary
A roller-coaster of a route that follows the watershed of the Yorkshire Dales.
Highest point: Whernside 2415'/736m
Lowest point: River Dee, Sedbergh 322'/98m

8 The M62 Roundabout

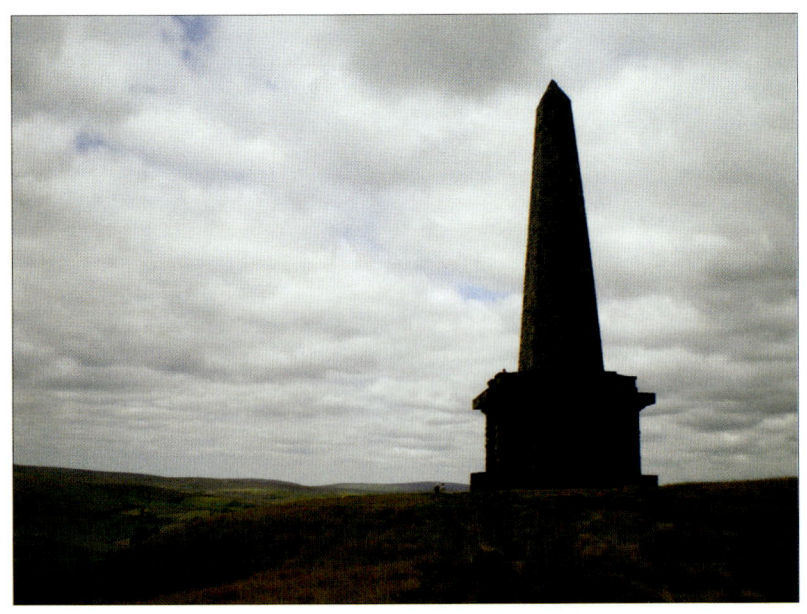

Stoodley Pike Monument

8 The M62 Roundabout

Distance: 40.25 miles/64.75km
Ascent: 7300'/2225m
Start & finish: Tunnel End car-park (SE 040 120)
Map: OS Explorer 1:25,000 OL21 South Pennines

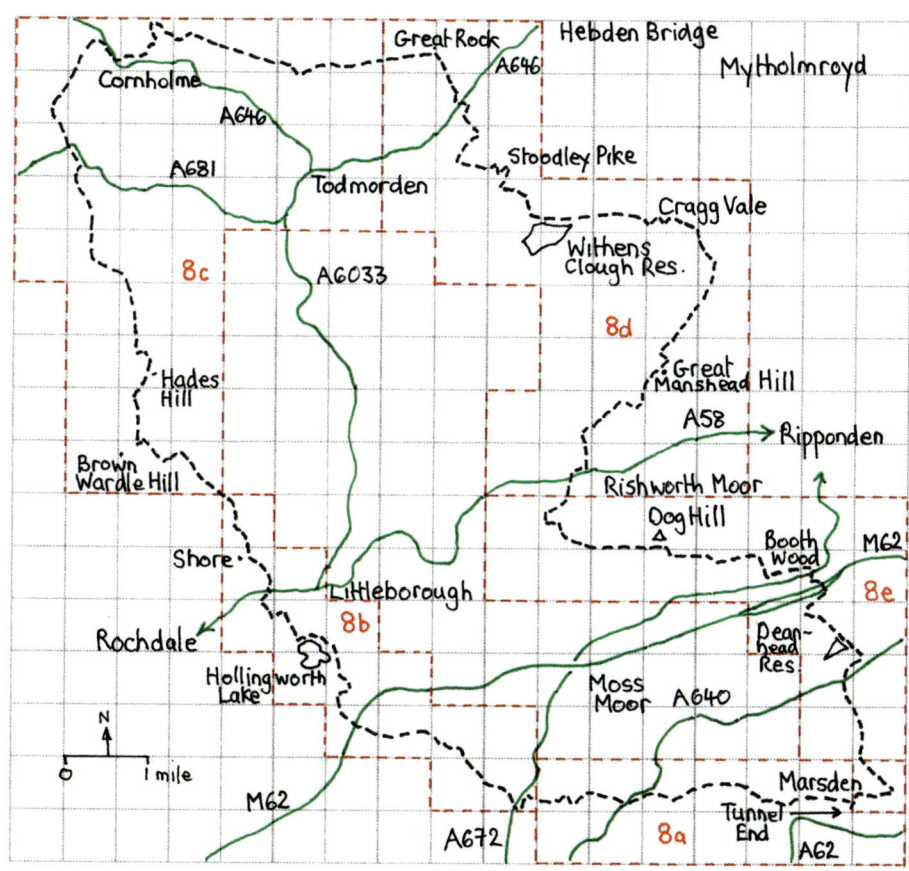

If the Pennine Chain is regarded as the backbone of England, then the Peak District, both in shape and position, has to be the pelvis. Surrounding this anatomical middle lie the guts of the North, a commercial jumble spawned by the greed of the Industrial Revolution. It didn't take long, as the towns of Lancashire and Yorkshire ballooned, for the grasping fingers of industry to claw into the countryside and kidnap the limited resources that would power their enterprise. Eventually only a small portion of green and brown remained and your walk jealously marches the bounds of a last oasis. Yet even this final wildness is now split by a direct blue vein bent on profit that, sweeping across Moss and Rishworth Moors, tackles the challenge that canal and rail had long evaded.

The proposed plans for the new motorway suggested it might prove an insurmountable obstacle to walkers, particularly those on the Pennine Way, which the M62 would sever, and for a short time it seemed there would be left no alternative but playing extreme hopscotch around the heavy traffic. Fortunately, the then Minister of Transport understood the needs of the outdoor world, so ordered a footbridge to be flung across the cutting being carved through Blackstone Edge. We, however, are trying to avoid that beaten track wherever possible, so look for a couple of ways not over but *under* this automated version of Pall Mall.

Our route, as its name implies, is a continuous loop that can be joined and left at any point of choice. The obvious points are Marsden, Littleborough and Hebden Bridge, each well served by public transport, but it suits my purposes to start and finish at the first-named or, to be more precise, at Tunnel End. The tunnel in question belongs to the Huddersfield Narrow Canal, which runs under the rough moors of Standedge to re-emerge blinking into the light of Diggle some three-and-a-quarter miles later. Its construction proved to be a major undertaking, not least because of a surveying miscalculation. In theory, the general idea was to start digging at each end and meet triumphantly in the middle. In practice, they were on course to miss each other and end up with two tunnels instead of one. Master builder Thomas Telford was called in to clear up the mess and eventually, after fifteen years of hard labour, the passage was completed.

You, too, have to cross Standedge but we keep to the open air. Leaving your support party at the Visitor Centre, where they can while away the time by taking a guided boat trip through the hillside, you set off in the general direction of Manchester. The initial road can, for the most part, be avoided by a pleasant riverside path until it begins to climb towards Lower Green Owlers, when a pack-horse route can be followed up Willy Kay Clough onto the high moors. As you would expect, the path uses the ground cleverly to maintain a rhythmic journey for beast and man and before long you have crossed the Pennine Way and the A672 before you take the plunge into the collage of reservoirs clustered above and between Denshaw and Ogden.

Once these are passed, M(auvais Pas)62 lies above. Unlike well-behaved children, this is first heard rather than seen as the ominous rumble of the modern-day pack-horses builds to a somewhat disturbing hum. As it turns out, the crossing is simplicity itself and, taking a leaf from the pages of the Huddersfield Narrow, is achieved by tunnelling beneath the elegant span of the motorway bridge. The dramatic effect of the moment is heightened as the bridge suddenly emerges behind the rising ground and ever increasingly towers over the walker. Now, for the first time, you can see where you are heading. Beneath your feet lie the local sports club (usually windswept), Hollingworth Lake (really a reservoir) and the town of Littleborough (the edge of civilisation as Mancunians know it). Beyond and on the horizon, the ridge of Brown Wardle Hill beckons.

If this were the sort of ground typical of a less inhabited part of Britain, the route would be obvious. Drop to the floor of the valley, cross the intervening span, then climb the opposite slope. On this occasion habitation intervenes. Despite its bravest efforts, our route can no longer keep a disdainful distance but must occasionally rub shoulders with the common herd. At first sight, there seems to be no alternative to mooching through the town's streets muttering platitudes to strangers, but a closer study of the map shows that it is possible to slide away from the main thoroughfares, over the canal and under the railway, to join the A58 at the Sun Inn. A streamside path followed by a right of way lead to the

King William IV, situated in the aptly named village of Shore. I delight in discovering these contrived and hidden ways. Perhaps they recall childhood reading of smugglers avoiding the various outposts of Authority or the excitement of solving a maze.

Provided you have not strayed off course into the adjacent mock Tudor, gig-lamped housing estates, with the attendant risk of being savaged by bands of roaming chihuahuas, you will quickly regain the high ground of a ridge that is followed from Brown Wardle towards Hades Hill. Whether this is a deliberate choice of name is not clear. But there is no doubt this area of Lancashire has a chequered history. As well as the legitimate business of mining for mineral deposits, a variety of nefarious practices took place among the mists—counterfeiting and the manufacture of illicit liquor being foremost among them. The *pièce de resistance*, however, was the shin-kicking contests between the representatives of nearby villages. The rules were simple. Men, stripped naked except for roughshod clogs, attempted to upend each other by the simple expedient of delivering violent blows to the shin. The sport has more or less died out in these parts, but has migrated to the more effete South where, emasculated through a combination of coyness and the current enthusiasm for Health and Safety, it has taken to wearing trousers stuffed with straw.

Around three miles later you cross the A681 and leave the Rossendale Way to drop into the next valley. In fact, the good burghers of Rossendale were not the only ones to come up with the idea of developing a rural sidewalk. Burnley, Todmorden and Calderdale have all come up with a similar scheme and have woven a collection of long-existing footpaths into Ways of their own. Our route mixes and matches to find its own way to Hebden Bridge and it should be acknowledged that if the existence of these official thoroughfares encourages the locals to join up the dots, it is a good thing. Not only is an ounce of fresh air worth a ton of Googled remedies but such regular exercise could have a greater effect of easing the burden on the NHS than any attempt by some Johnny-come-lately trying to make a political name for himself.

As you descend towards the A646 you pass a sign announcing a 'Welcome to Portsmouth', but don't be alarmed, you have

not lost your way—no three-masted man o' war is about to loom through the mist. After this curiously named village (what mouth of which port?) you follow a conglomeration of parochial pathways to the Great Rock. You may have noticed that since leaving Brown Wardle Hill you have effectively been following a parallel Pennine Way, with our next objective, the monument on Stoodley Pike, almost continually in view. The tower was originally built to commemorate the defeat of Napoleon but was destroyed by lightning on the eve of the Crimean War. Undeterred by such a portent, it was rebuilt to celebrate the charge of the Light Brigade. Little wonder these edifices are often described as 'follies'.

Great Rock (for those who feel their arms could do with a bit of exercise, there is a tricky little crack up the front and a veritable staircase at the back) signals a change of direction and the start of the long march home. A narrow lane leading east suggests the quickest way back to the valley but, as a notice points out to motorists, this is one of those moments when reliance on their Satnav can be somewhat optimistic. In my experience, the best form of digital expertise is to get someone who knows to point the way. Once down, duck under a railway bridge to reach Stoodley Glen across the Rochdale Canal. Despite the industrial wasteland near at hand, this seems a remote and secluded sort of spot and you can quickly get deliberately lost among the vegetation. Yet in hill walking, and contrary to much of the rest of life, what goes down must go up and it is a bit of a pull to reach high ground again. At around midway you cross a 'London Road', a reminder that the thoroughfares of road, rail and canal that lie beneath you are recent innovations and it was not that long ago that the valley bottom was far too marshy for any respectable traveller.

The summit gained, the next objective, Great Manshead Hill, comes into view. There is the inevitable rise and fall between it and you, and again seven-league boots seem the preferred option. But it is not as bad as it appears or, to put it another way, it could be considerably worse. After passing Withens Clough Reservoir and The Hinchcliffe, a rather fine little pub, the route reaches the B6138 at Cragg Vale. Fortunately, we cross this bit of the tarmac stretching from Mytholmroyd to Blackstone Edge Reservoir, at

a relatively high point. For this is the longest continuous stretch of uphill road in England, much sought after by trial cyclists and other such masochists. With this in mind, you step lightly across and after a relatively short pull reach the lanes that wind their way to your summit. You pass a couple of interesting buildings. First, a rather nice seventeenth-century house with a double-gabled frontage, then a squat brick-built affair which apparently was constructed to resemble something important and so confuse enemy bombers. As it seems in pretty good shape, it couldn't have been much of a decoy duck.

There are fine views towards the Peak District from the convenient seat at Manshead End and, although the most obvious way is to follow the discretionary path towards Baitings Reservoir, then a twisting of paths to Booth Wood, it is better to keep your height by descending in a more westerly direction and connecting with a good track that leads under Dog Hill to the same place. Mauvais Pas Mark 2 now beckons.

For some time you will have been aware of the motorway streaming across your path and there seems no obvious way of fording it. In fact, there is a route, as convoluted and contrived as that through Littleborough. Plunge off the main road, scuttle under the imposing rampart of Booth Wood Reservoir, then sneak through a couple of tunnels that burrow beneath the flood. In the middle of all this you will have passed Stott Hall Farm wedged between the two carriageways. The urban, or rather rural, myth has this as Farmer Custer's Last Stand against the townies, but the truth is less romantic. The partitioning of the M62 was more through geological necessity than eco-warrior defiance.

As we pass Deanhead Reservoir in another fall and rise to reach the A640, the thoughtful reader will have deduced at least two things about this particular route: a) it is a roller-coaster of a ramble and b) it passes an awful lot of water trapped in concrete. Nor are these two elements unconnected. The series of valleys radiating from the Pennines easily allow water to be collected in the hollows nestling between the ridges we've crossed. As the population grows, so will the demand for water and more reservoirs will have to be built, and it is a sobering thought that if it continues

at this rate, the prediction of W H Mitchell may well come true. Fifty years ago he suggested the whole area (in his case, the Lake District) would be submerged and surrounded by a motorway riding along the reservoir-retaining walls. A facility that, in times of sufficient drought, would allow the tourist to gape in awe at what were once the beauties of the English countryside.

As it turns out, Cupwith Reservoir, our final man-made pond, is more pastoral tarn than municipal monster and heralds the ideal end of the day. Before you, the moorland track first gives way to stony lanes, then eventually to the tarmac of Tunnel End and invites a gentle jog leading to a change of socks and an assortment of the vital fluids. But a word of warning—the final few yards are around the outskirts of some private herbaceous borders and, as all good mountaineers know, you are at your most vulnerable when you feel you are home and dry. After such mighty endeavour, it would be somewhat ignominious if you were to sustain an injury through tripping over a garden gnome.

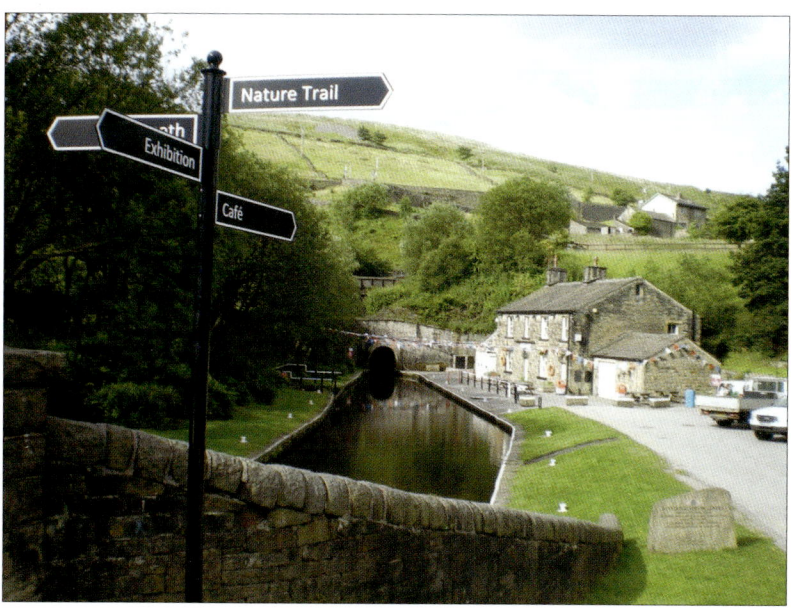

Tunnel End near Marsden

The M62 Roundabout Map 8a

Start: Tunnel End car-park (SE 040 120)
Finish: Near A672 (SD 980 122)
Distance: 4.25 miles/6.75km
Ascent: 1050'/320m

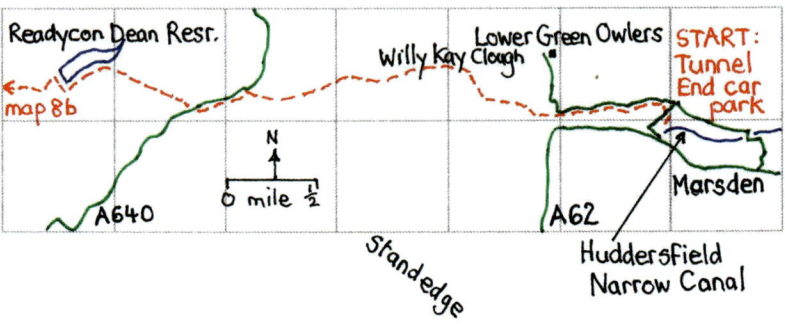

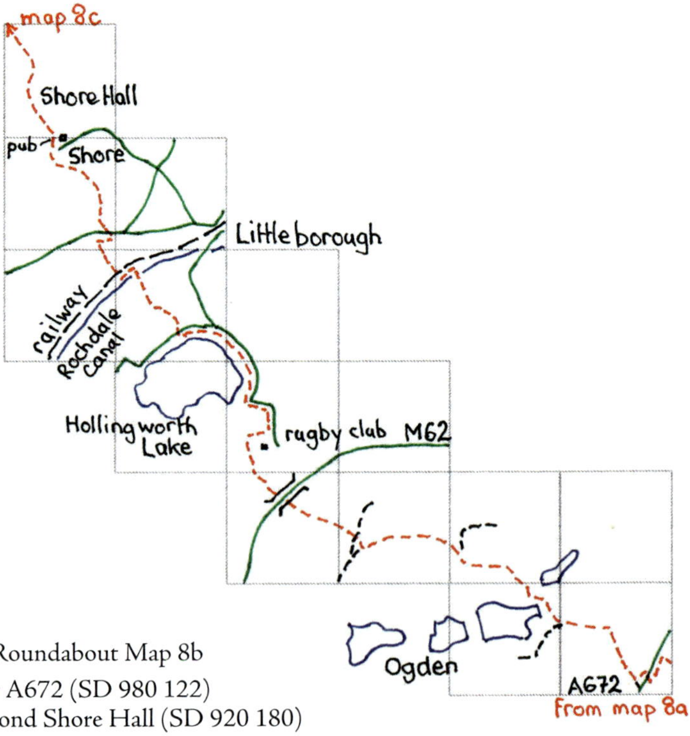

The M62 Roundabout Map 8b

Start: Near A672 (SD 980 122)
Finish: Beyond Shore Hall (SD 920 180)
Distance: 6.5 miles/10.25km
Ascent: 890'/271m

The M62 Roundabout Map 8c

Start: Beyond Shore Hall (SD 920 180)
Finish: West of Great Rock (SD 950 261)
Distance: 11 miles/17.75km
Ascent: 2,010'/613m

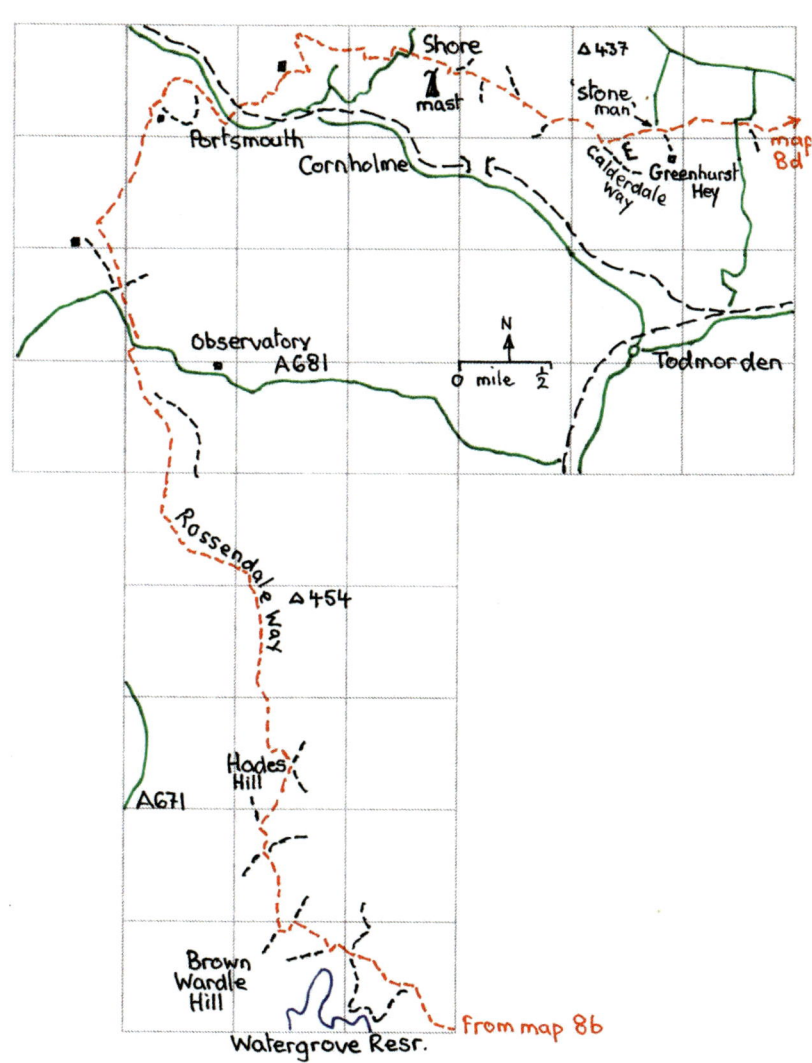

The M62 Roundabout Map 8d

Start: West of Great Rock (SD 950 261)
Finish: Roman Road near A58 (SD 985 180)
Distance: 10 miles/16.25km
Ascent: 2,070'/631m

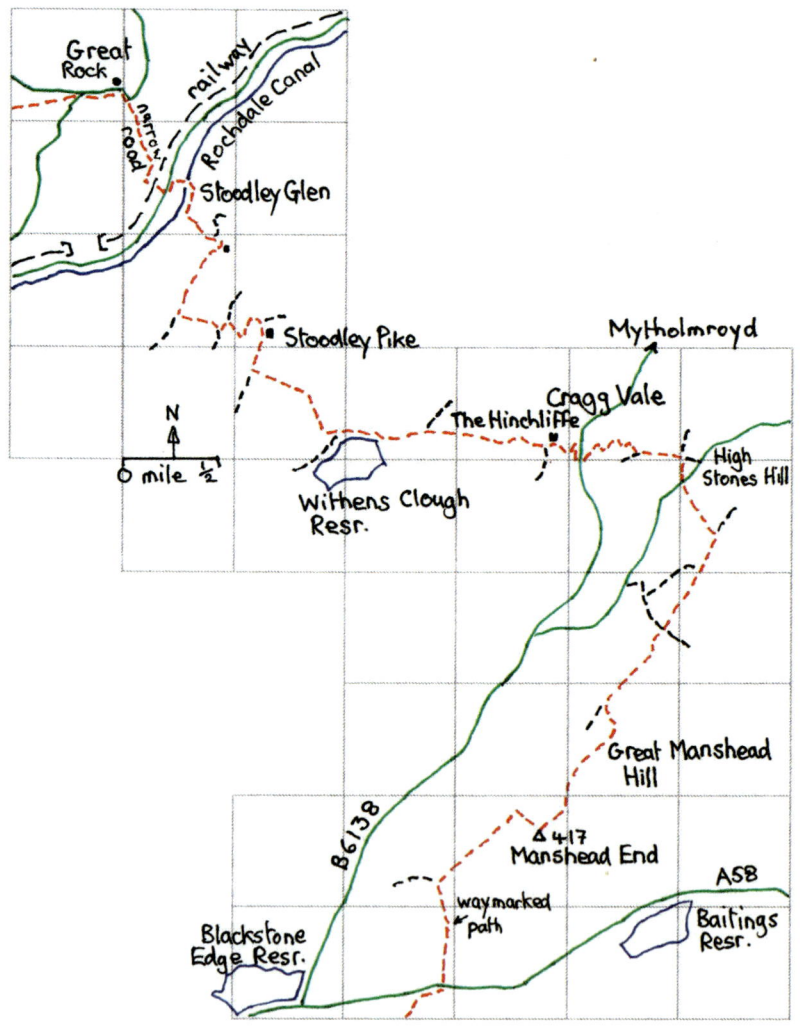

The M62 Roundabout Map 8e

Start: Roman Road near A58 (SD 985 180)
Finish: Tunnel End car-park (SE 040 120)
Distance: 8.5 miles/13.75km
Ascent: 1280'/390m

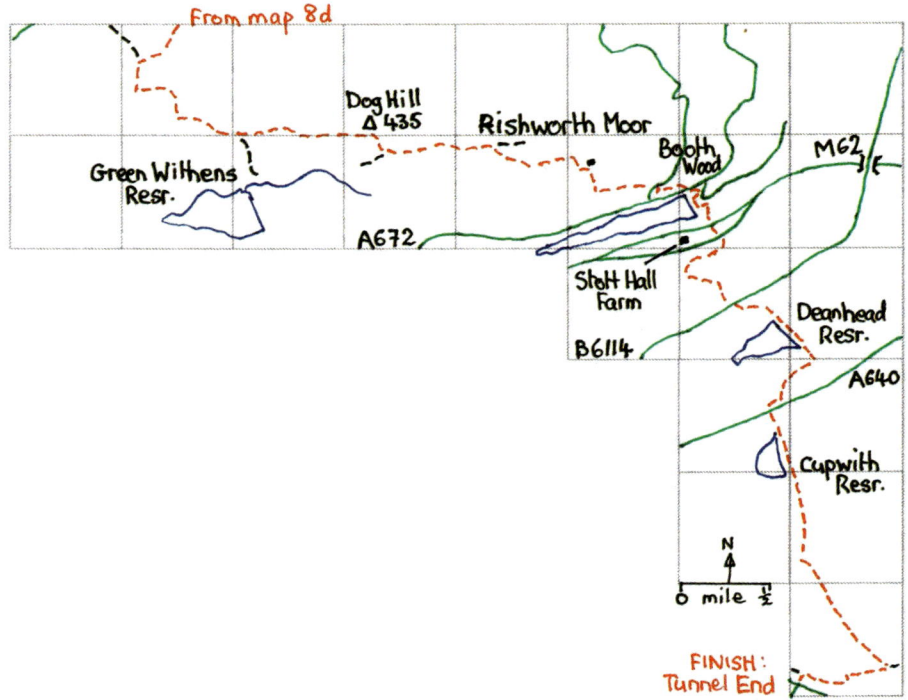

The M62 Roundabout Summary

Dodging the traffic to circle the interesting ground that lies between the satanic mills of south Lancashire and Yorkshire.

Highest point: Freeholds Top 1444'/440m
Lowest point: Rochdale Canal, near Todmorden 374'/114m

9 The Bakewell Pudding

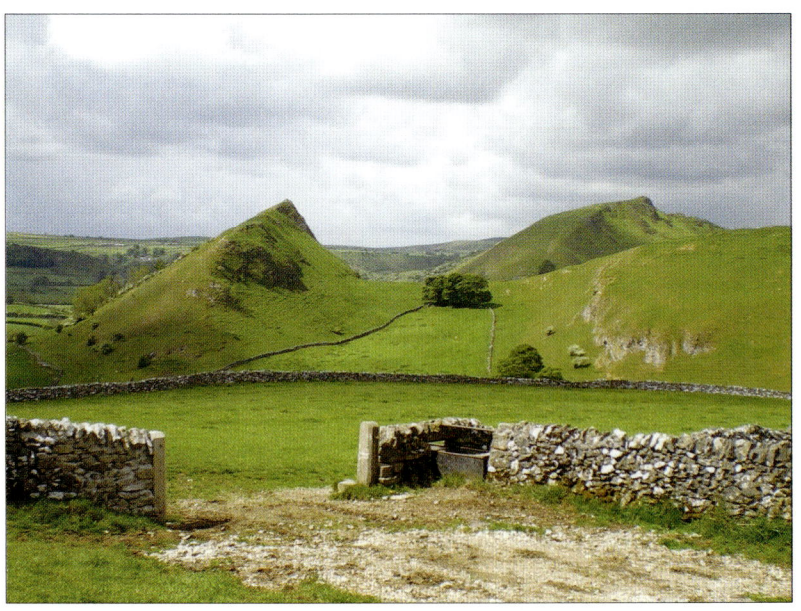

Parkhouse Hill and Chrome Hill

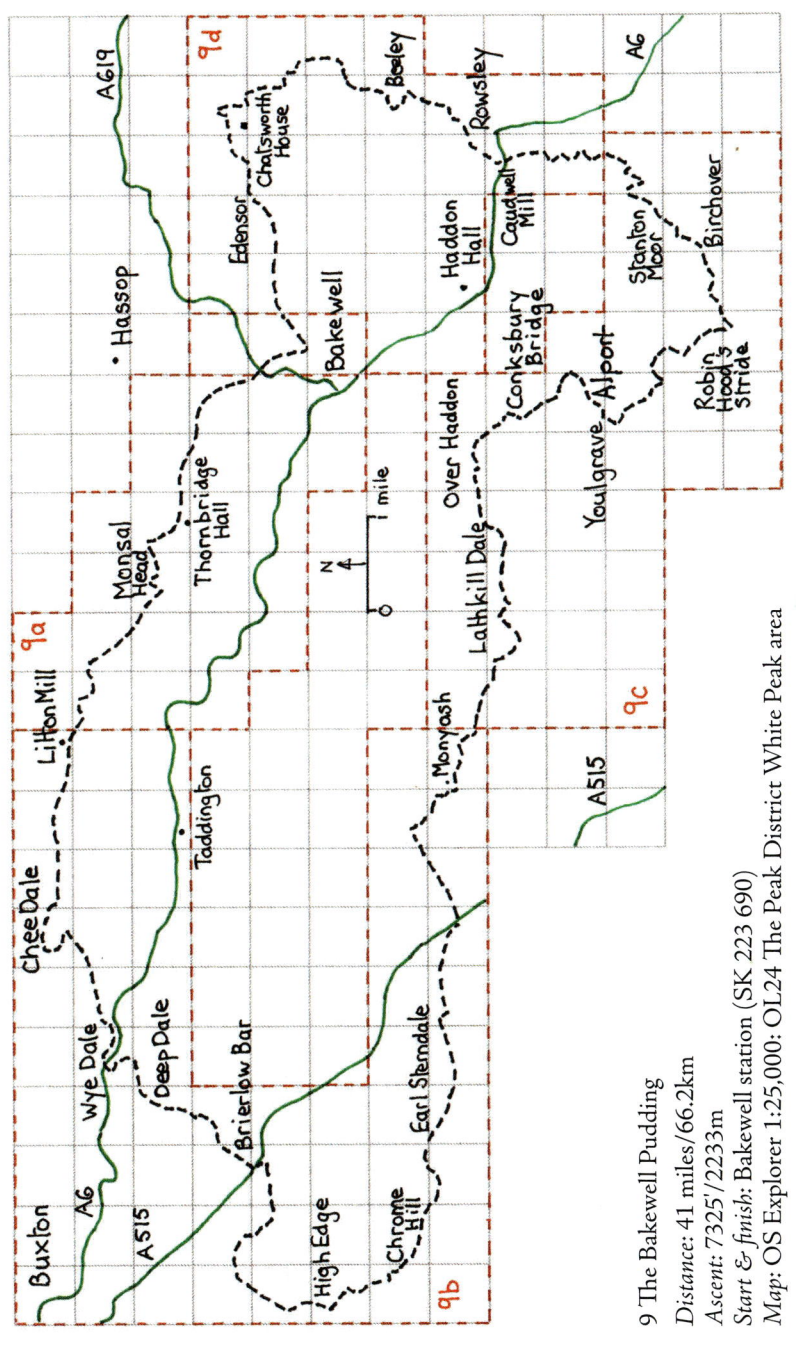

9 The Bakewell Pudding

Distance: 41 miles/66.2km

Ascent: 7325'/2233m

Start & finish: Bakewell station (SK 223 690)

Map: OS Explorer 1:25,000: OL24 The Peak District White Peak area

Pudding seems more than a little harsh. Mind you, Tart is scarcely an improvement. Here is a lighter touch, a soufflé perhaps, not found in the bogs and lings that characterise more northern moors. Whereas the horseshoe of grit that threatens to encircle our route is coarse-grained stuff, with rough, tough vegetation striving for breath in the peat, the limestone country through which we pass has pleasantly sprung grass and boasts towering white cliffs, often sunk in hidden valleys. If the gritstone edges thrust a fist aggressively against the skyline, the limestone tors, like refined ladies, seem to have tactfully withdrawn, the better to avoid the vulgarity of unnecessary display.

Mind you, this coyness often reveals unexpected pleasures. Perhaps it was the potential violation of these that caused John Ruskin to object when he heard of the proposed Buxton-to-Bakewell railway. In a letter entitled *Fors Clavigera*, addressed to the 'Workmen and Labourers of Great Britain', he lambasted the type of industrial entrepreneur that 'enterprised a railroad through the valley, blasted its rocks away, heaped thousands of tons of shale into its lovely stream' so that 'every fool in Buxton can be at Bakewell in half-an-hour, and every fool in Bakewell in Buxton'.

Our route starts at what remains of Bakewell station, which came into existence as a result of the race between railway companies competing to shift passengers and goods from the provinces to London. The Midland Railway put in a successful bid to run a line from Manchester, via Buxton and Matlock, and our walk initially follows its route along what is now known as the Monsal Trail. Rowsley, which we shall pass through later in the day, lies to the south and between there and our starting point the line had to pass the stately pile of Haddon Hall.

Unfortunately, its owner, the Duke of Rutland, decreed no train should approach within sight of his house, forcing the engineers to divert the route under his estate in a concealed tunnel. Not only was this nimbyism on a grand scale, but the diversion from the river plain also forced the inhabitants of Bakewell, regardless of age or infirmity, to toil up the steep hill of Station Road to catch the train on the outskirts rather than the more obvious location in the centre of town. Perhaps the Duke and Ruskin were in cahoots.

Or perhaps they were out of touch, for ever since Brunel realised that a station had a potential over and above its primary purpose, rail owners began to see that their points of entry and exit could be part of the glamour of travel. As a result, all stations had some redeeming flourish. Bakewell was no exception and sufficient remains to show it was once a most elegant structure. After the station is left, the old track, now Trail, passes through the remains of halts at Hassop and Thornbridge (built, no doubt, for the convenience of the inmates of those adjacent Halls) to reach the dividing wall of Monsal Head. Here you abandon the Trail and, rather than continue through the recently opened Headstone Tunnel, climb up via the old diversion to the Monsal Head Hotel. You will find this apparently unnecessary digression is entirely worthwhile. The view is justly famous and should not be missed, if only to appreciate the problems facing the Victorian engineers when they decided to balance a railway line along the tightrope of the Wye valley.

The former track twisted and turned on itself to make the best of what was left after the river had taken its share. Not surprisingly, these contortions involved a variety of bridges and tunnels and our route combines these artificial corridors with the natural paths that have roamed the valley for centuries. On a fine day there is little doubt that this section of the walk can appear idyllic, but close at hand there is a reminder of grimmer times. Litton Mill was owned by the notorious Ellis Needham who, because he was unable to attract local labour, took advantage of the Poor Law Act of 1601 to employ pauper children from the cities. These were treated as slaves, beaten and starved half to death, and often committed suicide to escape their misfortune. It was not until a journalist, John Brown, revealed the full extent of how this type of industrialist made his money that the practice came, let it be hoped permanently, to an end.

Today, any violent injury is more likely to be voluntarily inflicted. I have in my possession a photograph of a goods train travelling on the section of line between Bakewell and Buxton. The train is stationary and the driver, arms folded, is leaning out of the cab with his neck craned skywards. What had undoubtedly attracted

his attention was the sight of a figure, high above him, clinging to the cliff of the limestone gorge with no obvious means of support. Apparently even scheduled passenger trains would reduce speed to give the fare-paying passengers the chance of watching rock climbers going about their business. It might have been interesting to hear what Ruskin had to say about people who strip walls of loose rock and ivy for their own amusement. Fortunately, this guardian of artistic and moral values, though alive when rock climbing was in its infancy, was spared that particular sight.

There is no doubt the spectacle offered the occasional frisson of excitement. Unlike gritstone, which is usually sound, limestone is friable and generally unstable. Also, the angle tends to be very steep, so climbers were often off-balance and relied on their grip on the rock to keep them *in situ*. It did not take long for the pioneers to realise the traditional methods of grab and pull offered little in the way of dividends and, as a result, this kind of rock was initially left severely alone. It was not until 1950 that the likes of Graham West and similarly minded members of the Manchester Gritstone Climbing Club decided that climbing on gritstone was over-predictable and turned their attention to the Wye Valley with its imposing heights of Raven Tor and Plum Buttress.

It soon became clear that, if they didn't want to end up in a tangled heap listening to the sound of ambulance bells weaving their way along the A6, they would have to adopt different ethical tactics from those held by their predecessors. In this regard they held an in-built advantage, for, unlike the abstractions of the lawyers and clergymen who had dominated the early climbing scene, the newcomers had practical skills they could call upon. Among their trades was sheet-metal working and it was not long before they realised that an appropriate range of metal pegs and expansion bolts driven into the rock might give them a sporting chance of survival.

This heretical approach produced the inevitable howls of complaint fuelled by the usual mixture of prejudice and envy, but steadily the few became the many and when such internationally renowned celebrities as Joe Brown were seen constructing a girdle traverse of Chee Tor, the practice of ironmongery received the

official stamp of approval. The floodgates opened and by the turn of the century there were around 1500 routes in the Wye Valley alone and the improvement of technical skills, with the consequent diminution of reliance on artificial aid, means that the majority have now been climbed in the traditional manner. Admittedly, many of them are short in length, not much more than gymnastic problems, but some of the routes you will pass under, such as Sirplum and the Cornice, are clearly serious undertakings. And 'under' is the right word, for the 200 feet soaring above you may well overhang the path by several yards.

Once the stepping stones have been safely negotiated, the only immediate hazard is dodging the traffic as you cross the A6 to reach the mouth of Deep Dale. Follow that and its continuation, Back Dale, to Brierlow Bar, where a circuitous sweep above High Edge Raceway takes you to a minor road running under High Edge itself. What follows from this point to the village of Earl Sterndale is the surprise packet of the walk. Up to now you have been walking either through steep-sided valleys or over gently undulating arable land. At this point the land starts to assert itself in a quite dramatic fashion.

The ridge in front of you starts mildly enough, though a sense that the land is beginning to fall away on either side gives some indication of things to come, but after crossing another minor road on the way to Tor Rock, the change becomes more obvious. First, you may notice a mixing of grit and limestone, indicating that you are at the overlap of the Dark and White Peak. Second, the hill that confronts you is somewhat steeper than anything you have had to surmount so far. Chrome Hill and Parkhouse Hill are something of an anomaly in an area which, though called the Peak District, demonstrates a distinct shortage of the pointy stuff. So much so that cynics only familiar with the likes of Kinder Scout and Bleaklow might suggest Plateau District as a more apposite name.

But such dismissive condescension cannot apply to the District as a whole. Once the limestone climbs out of the valleys, it forms not only distinct summits but also narrow ridges with impressive drops on either side. While not in the same league as the Skye

Cuillin or the Aonach Eagach, the traverse along the summit ridges of Chrome Hill and Parkhouse Hill can be made quite as exciting as Sharp Edge or anything else the Lake District has to offer. This full crossing is a relatively recent possibility for, although there has been a concessionary path across Chrome Hill for some time, it was not until 19th September 2004 that Access legislation allowed us complete freedom to roam on Parkhouse and the traverse of these two fine ridges to be combined. You return to earth at Earl Sterndale, where the most interesting feature, apart from the pub, is the church which, set amid ancient gravestones, seems unreasonably modern. The explanation is simple. St Michael & All Angels was the only Derbyshire church to be substantially damaged by enemy bombs and was not restored until 1952.

The route leaves from the front of The Quiet Woman (the inn's sign explains all) and sets off to complete the southern section as far as the Druid Inn at Birchover, where it once more turns north. In truth, with the Royal Oak at Sparklow, the Bull at Monyash and being spoiled for choice at Youlgrave, you could easily turn this section into a pub crawl. An ambition probably best kept for another occasion. But this plethora is also something of an anomaly. On a round of the Bakewell Pudding you could, if you wished, easily visit a dozen or more pubs en route. The other eight walks put together could scarcely muster that number. Yet alcoholic opportunity is not the only thing that's changing. Something more general is afoot.

You begin to realise what's happening as you follow the ridge running between Earl Sterndale and Monyash. From this vantage point you can look south and see land that rolls, rather than falls, into the river valleys. This easing of the landscape allows an increase in sites suitable for habitation and a proliferation of roads to allow greater access. Net result—more houses, more pubs. Here, as on Kerridge Ridge during the first of our walks, we have once more reached the edge of the more abstemious northern hills. Moreover, compared with the moors of Durham, the land we are crossing is strollers' country, a mixture of field paths and good tracks presenting an ideal opportunity for stretching your legs and slaking your thirst. And it is not just the land that

changes. Accents become flatter, with the sound coming from the front rather than the back of the mouth. Vowels adopt a native hue, as I discovered when my pronunciation of 'Chrome Hill' was sharply corrected to 'Chroom'.

Once through Monyash, the route, not for the first time, draws back the curtain on another of its spectacles when, from relatively flat farmland, it suddenly disappears down its own rabbit-hole. This Alice in Wonderland transformation is the beginnings of Lathkill Dale, one of the finest of its kind in Derbyshire. It may not be as dramatic as the Wye valley, but eventually even towering limestone cliffs can become much of a muchness. There is, at first, no sign of the inevitable stream which, like most limestone rivers, spends part of its journey underground. If the weather has been wet, it will first appear out of the mouth of Lathkill House Cave. If not, it may be over half a mile later before there is any sign of water. As with the chameleon, the character of the valley changes as you progress. Sides become steeper and sturdier trees flanked by a profusion of wild flowers start to colonise the steep banks.

It is when it is joined by the waters from Cales Dale, that you begin to understand why Izaak Walton, in *The Compleat Angler*, singles out the Lathkill as 'by many degrees, the purest and most transparent stream that ever yet I saw, either at home or abroad'. Further downstream, near the village of Over Haddon, there are signs of earlier industrial development and in a dry summer the river can once more disappear underground. These two sights are not unconnected. The workings of the lead mines you have just seen have considerably lowered the water table and in some summers the river may not reappear until Over Haddon is passed. The dale, ever more deeply foliaged, continues under the bridge that once served the now deserted medieval village of Conksbury, before being joined by the River Bradford at Alport. Here we leave it to pick up a section of the Limestone Way, which is followed until the time comes to branch off towards Birchover.

It takes no more than a cursory glance at an OS map to realise that the land between Birchover and Rowsley has been long regarded as spiritually significant. We have already passed by two sets of standing stones and close to a hermit's cave built into the

cliff at Cratcliffe Tor, enough to suggest that all this area might once have been considered sacred ground. Legend, moreover, has it that Rowtor Rock was once a Druid temple, a myth given substance by the labyrinth of tunnels, steps and terraces carved out of the stone. The truth is more prosaic. The Tor stands in the garden of what was the vicarage and it was only at the end of the seventeenth century that the Rev William Ellis created these improvements for his own amusement.

Regardless of legend, it's clear Birchover has been around for a long time. Not only have Bronze Age barrows been excavated and evidence found of Roman and Saxon remains, but entries in the Doomsday Book and the Derbyshire Charter show that it continued to maintain its significance through the centuries. To this very day, visitors to London are reminded of the village's place in history as both the Tower of London and Houses of Parliament contain the much sought-after Birchover stone.

The route to Rowsley passes over Stanton Moor and through the pleasantly wooded Nine Ladies Stone Circle. The ladies in question are believed to have been turned into stone for dancing on Sunday, but the pillars undoubtedly go back further than the enforcement of patriarchal Christianity. What with voiceless women and petrified maidens, it is clear the feminine cause hereabouts had a long and hard road to travel. Once the moor is crossed, you drop, with fine views of the Derwent Valley, to Caudwell's flour mill (an excellent working example of the use of water as a source of power) and further traffic-dodging on the A6.

As with any circular route, there is always an opportunity to cut an odd corner or two and there is no doubt that from Rowsley the shortest way home is to follow the River Derwent as far as Beeley, then swing left under New Piece Wood to regain the Monsal Trail. But the strength of this walk is its diversity, so we decided to include a short detour through the grounds of Chatsworth House. It is generally agreed the much admired gardens are a splendid reflection of the skills of Capability Brown, but the parkland you negotiate, with the skilful placing of trees to allow unobtrusive felling and manipulation of the river's course to create a network of drainage, more subtly shows the expertise of his guiding hand.

Once the farm and the House itself have been passed, it is a short step through Edensor and its adjoining lanes to reach once more Bakewell station.

There is also a more important reason for the detour through Chatsworth land. There are a number of rights of way passing over the grounds and there have been moments in the past when the estate and the general public have not seen eye to eye over the question of rights and responsibilities. Such was the disagreement that the Highway Authority of Derbyshire was the last to produce the required Definitive Map of the footpaths in the area. This, with the newly formed access to Parkhouse Hill, should remind us how hard won was the battle for the common man to regain the use of what had always been his. We have also seen enough on this collection of walks to realise there are those who would like to turn back the proprietorial clock if they could, so it is incumbent on us all to make certain these rights are neither taken for granted nor eroded through neglect.

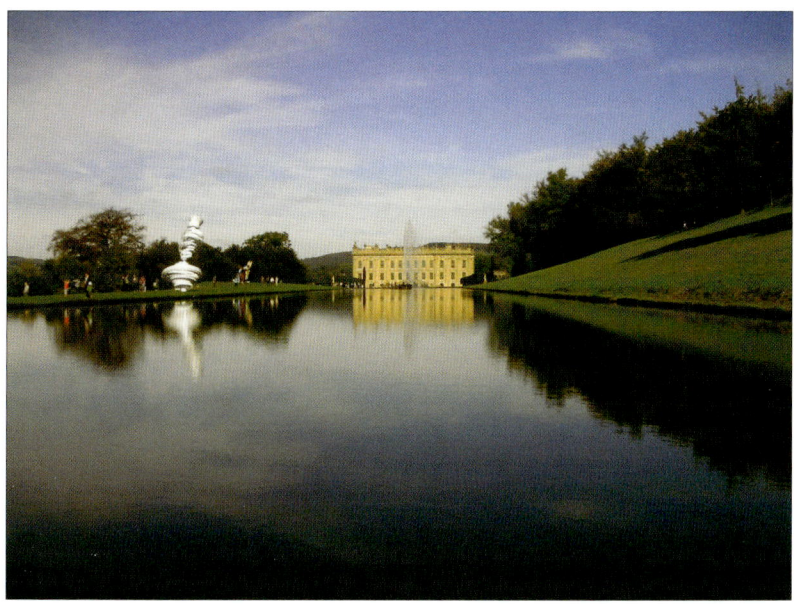

Emperor Fountain at Chatsworth during annual Sculpture Exhibition

The Bakewell Pudding Map 9a

Start: Bakewell station (SK 223 690)
Finish: Monsal Trail above
Litton Mill (SK 160 729)
Distance: 5.5 miles/8.9km
Ascent: 900'/274m

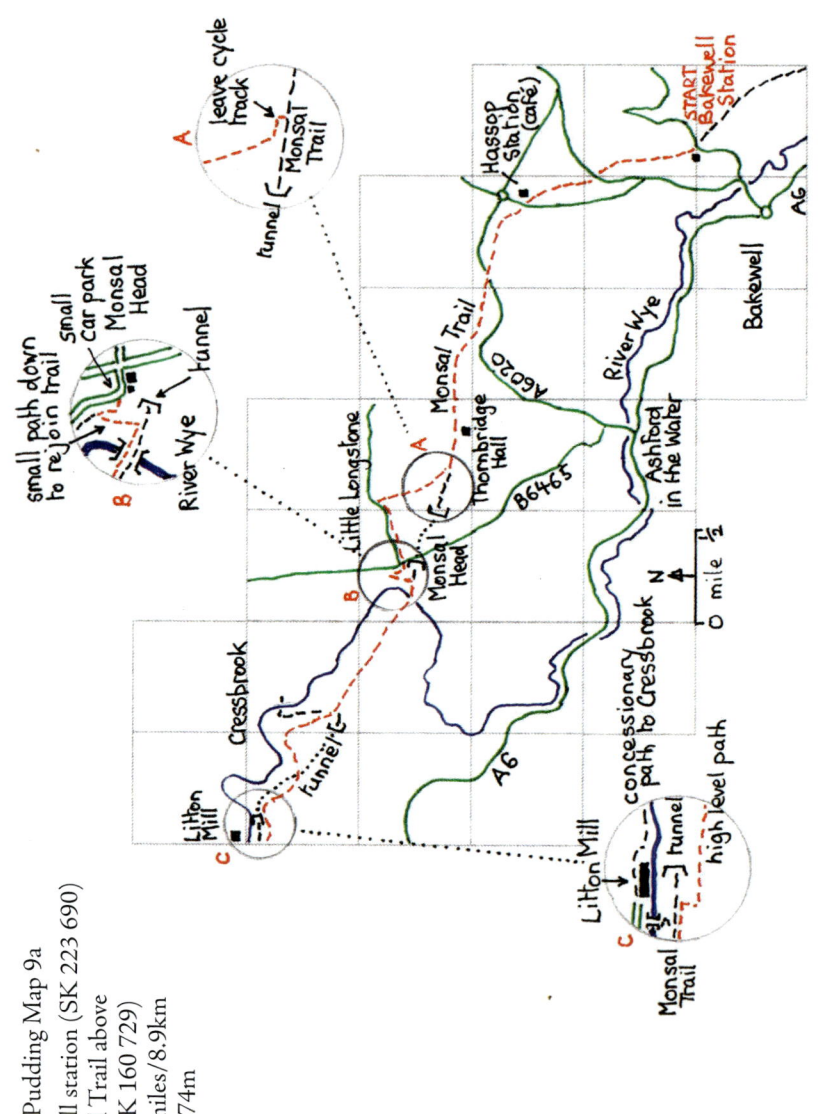

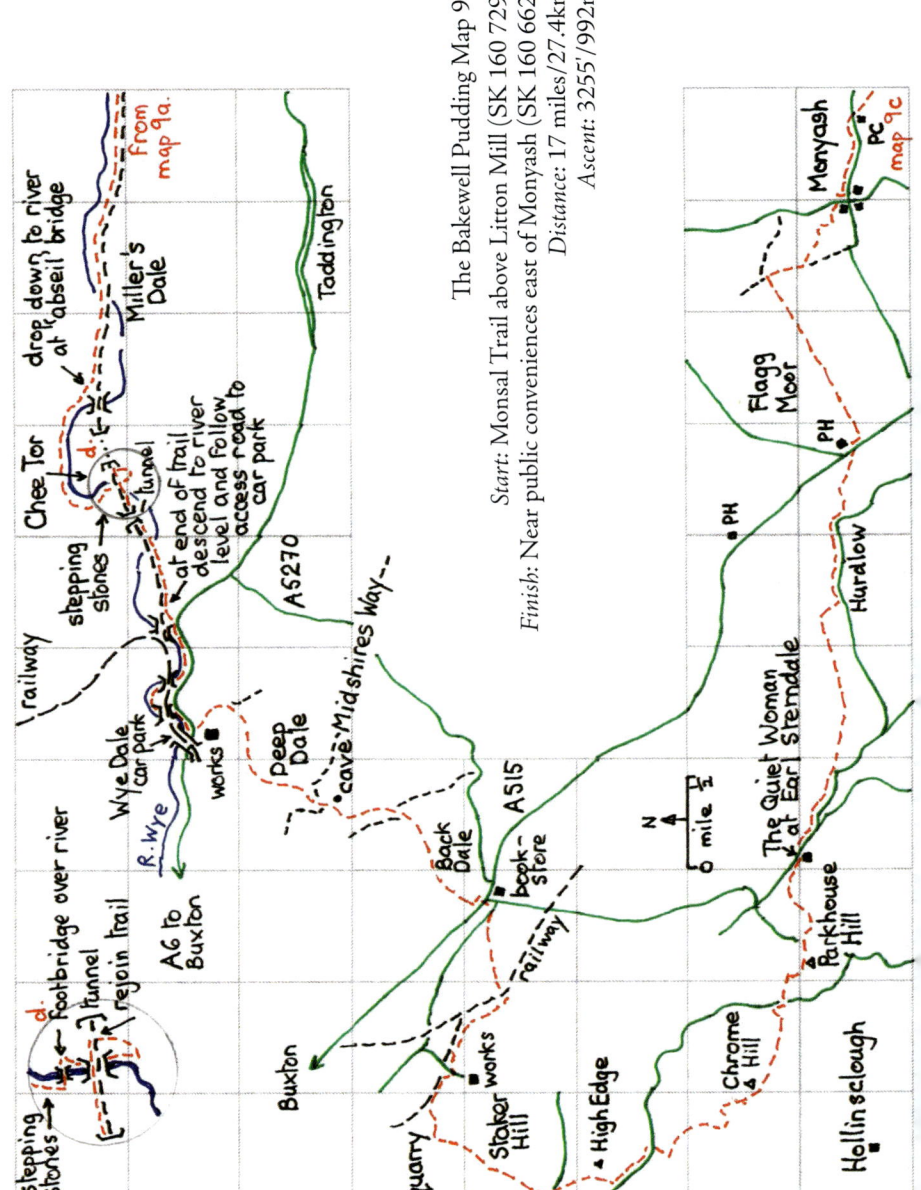

The Bakewell Pudding Map 9b

Start: Monsal Trail above Litton Mill (SK 160 729)
Finish: Near public conveniences east of Monyash (SK 160 662)
Distance: 17 miles/27.4km
Ascent: 3255'/992m

The Bakewell Pudding Map 9c

Start: Near public conveniences east of Monyash (SK 160 662)

Finish: Near Hillcarr Wood (SK 225 640)

Distance: 10.25 miles/16.6km

Ascent: 1755'/535m

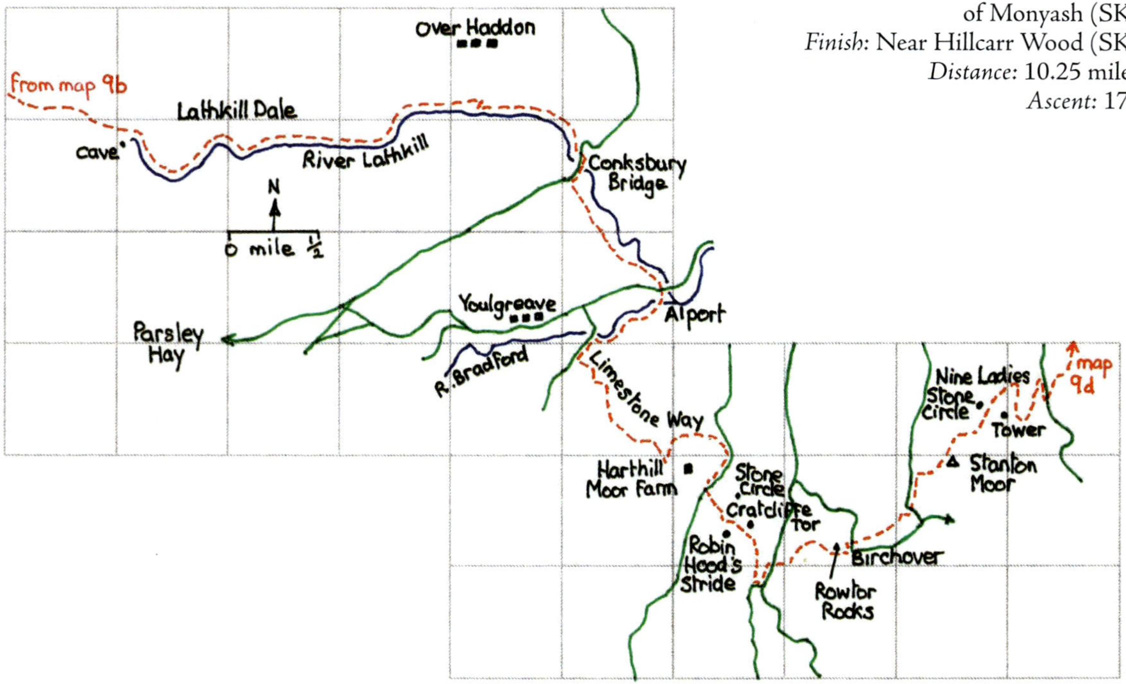

from map 9b

Over Haddon

Lathkill Dale

River Lathkill

Cave

N

0 mile ½

Parsley Hay

Conksbury Bridge

Alport

Youlgreave

R. Bradford

Limestone Way

Harthill Moor Farm

Robin Hood's Stride

Stone Circle

Cratcliffe Tor

Rowtor Rocks

Birchover

Nine Ladies Stone Circle

Tower

Stanton Moor

to map 9d

119

The Bakewell Pudding Map 9d

Start: Near Hillcarr Wood
(SK 225 640)
Finish: Bakewell station
(SK 223 690)
Distance: 8.25 miles/13.3km
Ascent: 1415'/432m

The Bakewell Pudding Summary

A delightful journey that connects the best of the White Peak. The going is easy, with no shortage of points of refreshment.

Highest point: High Edge, near Buxton 1476'/450m
Lowest point: River Derwent, Rowsley 318'/97m

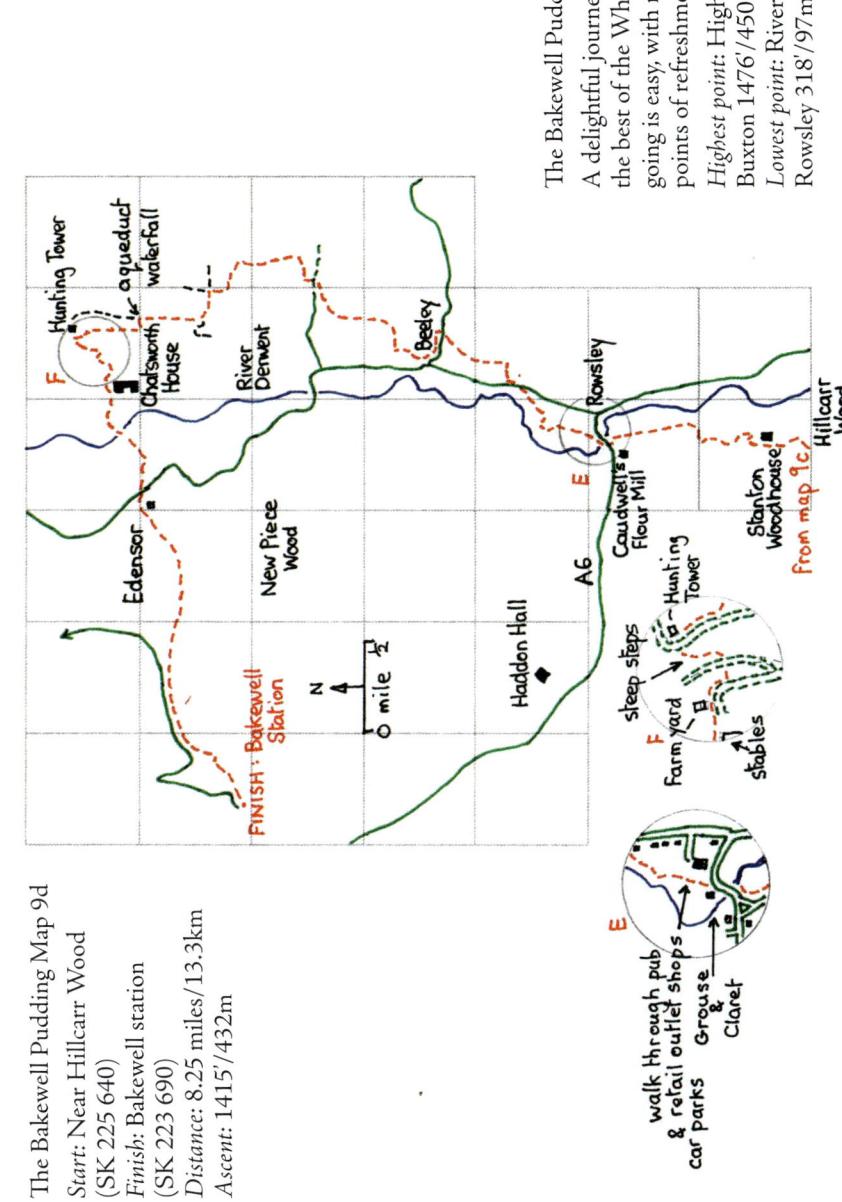

120

Baggers and Trotters

The story of long-distance walking in the North of England

People have, from time immemorial, walked long distances. Commercial travellers, itinerant preachers and North Country shepherds have all, in their lines of business, covered many miles in a single journey. I can even remember my great aunt telling me that, to reach the equivalent of her primary school, she had to walk five miles there and five miles back on a daily basis. The reaction of some of today's pupils, if the 4x4 does not pull up within five yards of the school gate, is probably best left unsaid. Yet it's not simply a question of walking long distances. What counts in any history of long-distance challenge walking, is to discover the point when people started walking for recreation, not in the sense of a romantic stroll, with probably ulterior motives, but to experience the pleasure of a sporting challenge in the hills.

Of the journeymen mentioned above, the Lakeland shepherd is the nearest to the modern day fell-walker, covering similar terrain at a pace that is deliberately measured. So it is a happy coincidence that a round of Wasdale, starting from Scafell and ending at Stirrup Crag, came to be regarded as something of a hill-walking record. Nor is it a surprise that this feat of nine separate summits in a day was completed by a clergyman, the Rev J M Elliot, a member of a profession which seems to have been at the forefront of pioneering mountain ascents. (Perhaps it was a case of 'Nearer, my God, to Thee'.) More relevantly, if this is to be taken as an example of an early challenge walk, it is reasonable for us to assume, at least in 1864, that any record attempt was judged by a combination of distance covered and peaks climbed.

An alternative to this type of challenge was to attempt a set of hills that shared some common denominator. In the case of the Lakes, the obvious such choice was the ascent of the fells over 3000 feet. In such cases, as the combination of peaks climbed and distances travelled was constant, the only variant of note was the time taken, so it began to be recognised that, for any such round to count, it should be completed within 24 hours. There must

still have been some debate as to which set of rules governed a 'proper' challenge, but the matter seemed to have been resolved in 1905 when, as mentioned in the Introduction, Dr A W Wakefield completed a round, starting and finishing at Keswick, in 22 hours seven minutes.

On the strength of that, he declared that to break his record, a contestant, starting and finishing at the same point, would have to complete a similar route, climbing, within 24 hours, a greater number of peaks over 2000 feet. There is no doubt his was an impressive effort and as his route became the skeleton around which Bob Graham's iconic round and its successors were built, it is worth noting in detail the peaks ascended. These were: Robinson, Hindscarth, Dalehead, Grey Knotts, Brandreth, Green Gable, Great Gable, Kirk Fell, Pillar Fell, Steeple, Red Pike, Yewbarrow, Scafell, Scafell Pike, Ill Crag, Great End, Esk Pike, Bowfell, Fairfield, Dollywagon Pike, Helvellyn, Saddleback and Skiddaw.

Although Wakefield's 'rules' were probably in line with common practice, they, nevertheless, imposed a structure on any future attempt. The minimum height of 2000 feet meant there were no easy peaks to add to your bag at the beginning or end of the course. The use of the full 24 hours meant you had to plan with some care where you were going to spend the hours of darkness—you didn't want to find yourself on Broad Stand or descending a steep pathless scree slope in the pitch black. Furthermore, you couldn't boost the tally by starting or finishing at the top of two different mountains. But, whatever the 'rules', it was a long way round, a distance exaggerated by an enthusiastic press that put it at '90 miles; equivalent to nearly 120'. People thought about it, then thought again and almost a couple of decades passed before it was officially accepted that Wakefield's record had been beaten.

Although it had the greater reputation, the Lake District was not the only place where people indulged in arduous walking over difficult northern terrain. Some sixteen years after the Rev Elliot's seminal effort, the Manchester YMCA Rambling Club was formed. It encouraged its members to explore the neighbouring Peak District from the west and it wasn't long before a counter-

invasion arrived from the east, spearheaded by G H B Ward, the formidable leader of the Sheffield Clarion Ramblers. There was no doubt that, between the fellbaggers in the Lakes and the bogtrotters, as they came to be known, in the Peak, a large-scale competitive sport was about to evolve.

There were, however, real differences between what happened in Derbyshire and the activities in the more northern fells. Unlike the relatively well-heeled residents of the Wasdale Head Hotel, the majority of those who visited the likes of Kinder and Bleaklow lived in the inner cities and it was all they could afford to take a tram from the town centre to the edge of the countryside. Rather than a leisurely fortnight in the Lakes, the best they could hope for was a few rushed hours in the fresh air. Not for them the pleasure of stretching their legs across the close-cropped turf and well-worn paths of the fells, rather a winding among a featureless wilderness of bogs and mosses that often required tiresome detours and, when the mist came down, careful navigation.

They soon learnt the best way to cover such ground was not in heavily nailed boots but wearing footwear which was as light as possible and, rather than plod, to try to skim over the surface. This meant they could cover long distances in a relatively short time. It also offered a more covert advantage. Unlike the fells surrounding Wasdale, access to most of the grouse moors of the Peak was generally prohibited and the land was fiercely guarded by keepers employed by the estate owners. Evasion was the name of the game but, if confrontation threatened, even the most belligerently armed bailiff must have thought twice when faced by a motley dressed band charging down a hillside at full pelt.

Inevitably, this level of fierce mutual support among a large number of people meant competition was keen and long-distance challenges would be made and met. But just as the Lakes had relied on Wakefield to lead the charge to greater things, so the Peak had to wait for a similar champion to emerge. Cecil Dawson was a Manchester cotton merchant whose reputation in the Peak soon became widespread. He was a powerful walker and, before he got into his stride over Derbyshire's bogland, once walked from Llandudno to Manchester accompanied by his luggage in a pony

and trap. Dawson completed the journey. The pony did not. His *tour de force* was the development of the Marsden to Edale walk, a tough 25-mile high-level walk across the three peaks of Black Hill, Bleaklow and Kinder Scout. Clearly, even this was not far enough for him, as it was not long before he doubled the distance by starting at Colne and finishing at Buxton.

The Colonel, as he was known, roamed the area with a band of friends (Dawson's 94th), outwitting keepers and pushing distances always that little bit farther. Unlike the Lakes, where the long-distance walks were generally circular, the big challenges in the Peak were point to point, usually ending in a town with a railway station. The attraction of the Marsden/Edale, for example, was that you left Manchester on the Huddersfield line and returned home on the Sheffield. Moreover, because trains are as unforgiving as time or tide, the restrictions of work meant the 24-hour limit so favoured in the Lakes was far less important than the demands of your employer. In the Peak the allotted time span for most long-distance walks was the interval between finishing work on Saturday morning and catching the last train home on Sunday night.

It is difficult to estimate how much interaction existed between walkers in the Lakes and their counterparts in the Peak. There may have been a certain amount of rivalry and, perhaps, even mutual disdain. Dawson in 1916 attempted to better Wakefield's round. Although he added two extra peaks and a further six miles to the doctor's tally, he took ten minutes longer and, much to his disgust, his efforts were not accepted as being an improvement on the standing record. But if there was a certain amount of antipathy between the two camps, one man emerged who would bridge the gap. As the Introduction suggests, Eustace Thomas appeared an unlikely candidate but was clearly driven by some inner fury.

He set about repeating all of Dawson's great through-routes but, influenced by the concept of the round so favoured in the Lakes, Thomas decided to construct one of his own. The Derwent Watershed is around 40 miles and religiously crosses every stream at its source, a route which involves some very rough country and more than a few frustrating detours. At the same time, he had his

eye on Wakefield's record and, after an initial failure, finally suc-
ceeded in 1920. A detailed and interesting account of his prepara-
tions, both physical and psychological, is to be found in the 1922
Journal of the Fell & Rock Climbing Club.

Remarkably, after successfully completing the round, Thomas
took a short rest before continuing his journey to add several
more peaks in the Grasmoor range, only calling it a day when he
reached a total height of 30,000 feet. He then withdrew to the
Alps and left the field open for others. But nothing of note seems
to have happened on the Cumbrian Fells until, in 1932, another
walk around the Lakes markedly upped the ante. On 13th June
Bob Graham set out from Keswick's market place and within 24
hours had returned to his starting point, having ascended 42 peaks,
one for each year of his age. His route followed the general course
of Wakefield's round but, instead of descending to Grasmere, he
included the Langdale Pikes and crossed the A591 at the high
point of Dunmail Raise.

Again, there were wild estimates in the Press of the distance
travelled and height ascended but, in fact, although the increase
on Wakefield's record looked spectacular, it was not quite as great
as the numbers would suggest. By keeping his height after Bowfell,
Graham picked up not only the Langdales, but also another five
peaks that lay on route, including two that did not reach the
height Wakefield had stipulated. After Helvellyn, Graham again
maintained his height and collected six extra and easily available
peaks before reaching Threlkeld. It was, nevertheless, a tremen-
dous effort and was not repeated for 28 years.

Further south, meanwhile, geography dictated the challenges of
the Colne/Rowsley and the Derwent Watershed were the nearest
the Peak could get to the Graham Round. So efforts were concentrated on faster times or, with the likes of the Marsden/Edale,
double crossings. A variant was completing old routes under
winter conditions. The only real novelty was an extension of the
1922 Three Inns Walk (Cat and Fiddle, Snake and Isle of Skye)
by including other hostelries, notably the George and Dragon,
Woodhead, the Flouch, Hazlehead and the Nag's Head at Edale.
One reason for this apparent lack of fresh challenges may have

been that, at the time, the real efforts in the Peak were directed elsewhere. Among the repercussions of the First World War was an assertion of individual rights and a rise in left-wing politics. Access for the many over the vast areas of land owned by the few was high on the agenda and fierce battles took place between walkers and keepers, culminating in the Mass Trespass of 1932 with the imprisonment of the ringleaders. Records could wait. More serious issues were in hand.

It was not until 1953 that a route appeared in the Peak to equal the Bob Graham. As hinted above, only a combination of the existing challenge walks would allow the Peak to provide such a rival, if not in picturesque splendour, at least in difficulty. In 1953, 'Larry' Lambe and John Sumner set out to complete a route now known as The Horseshoe of the Peak. This 60+ mile tramp followed the outside edge of the gritstone rim that embraces the limestone of the White Peak. It started at Hen Cloud and, keeping to the high ground, incorporated the toughest part of the Derwent Watershed before following the gritstone edges to finish at Matlock. This first attempt, blighted by miserable weather and an injury to Lambe's Achilles tendon, took 37 hours ten minutes but, under the right conditions, it was clearly a candidate for a 24-hour challenge.

It was now becoming obvious that, like many athletic activities, these long-distance challenges were following a particular pattern. Stage one sorted out the general ground rules. Stage two, an outstanding individual (in the case of the Lakes, Wakefield) sets a bench-mark for would-be aspirants. Stage three, a general catching up, whereupon, stage four, an outstanding individual (Graham) once again raises the bar and so on, apparently *ad infinitum*. A similar state of affairs occurred in the Peak, with first Dawson and then Lambe as the pace-setters. But, as the second half of the century gained momentum, for most of the pundits there was only one show in town. The Bob Graham Round! And who would be the first to repeat it?

An early attempt had been made in 1933 by F Spencer Chapman, anxious to return the record to Sedbergh School, Wakefield's and his Alma Mater. Despite a valiant effort, he finished an hour outside the allotted time. There were other close efforts but it was

not until the Heaton brothers, Alan and Ken, appeared on the scene that it looked as if the inevitable would finally happen. Together with Stan Bradshaw, a fellow member of the Clayton-le-Moors Harriers, they set off from Keswick on Saturday 25th June 1960, determined to succeed where others had failed. It was not a trouble-free round. The temperature soared steadily, a supporter accidentally broke Ken's glasses, leaving him virtually blind, and Bradshaw suffered badly from cramp. Only Alan kept going sufficiently well to surpass Graham's time by more than an hour.

In his book, *In Mountain Lakeland*, published in 1963, Harry Griffin expanded on an earlier newspaper article in which he had introduced the exploits of Bob Graham to the public at large. This acted as a spur and two types of contestant emerged. The first was a group which was more than happy just to complete the round within 24 hours, but the second saw it as an individual challenge and set out to record ever faster times. There was also a subdivision of this last group who decided to add more peaks within the 24 hours and so make a 'Round' of their own. Ken Heaton pushed it up to 51, his brother then added three more. Joss Naylor, with first 60 and then 72, put clear water between himself and rivals. As the century ended, Mark Hartell achieved a total of 77 and completed the standard round in less than fifteen hours.

With the constraints of geography and the obvious challenges completed, the question is, what's next? Of course, individuals can add more peaks, walk greater distances, record faster times, but is there still an opportunity to create a new type of challenge walk? One possibility is to reduce multi-day routes to a single 24-hour journey. Unsurprisingly, Joss Naylor was the first to investigate such a possibility, completing Wainwright's Coast to Coast in 40 hours. He than turned his attention to that author's greatest work, the series of volumes entitled *The Pictorial Guide to the Lakeland Fells*. Wainwright had divided these into separate sections, listing all the summits in each area. Although there seems to be no hard or fast rule as to the nature of a top, the collection has become, in the eyes of many, the definitive list of hills in the District.

The author had chosen his divisions well, for each book contained roughly the same number of hills and, as there were seven

books in all, it was not long before it was realised that Wainwright had created a challenge of truly Biblical proportions. A book a day for seven days and Lo! It would come to pass. Predictably, Naylor took up the challenge and in 1987 completed the lot at an average of around 30 peaks a day. In one sense, walking in the Lakes had come full circle. It would have been the local dalesmen who first showed the aspiring poets and Alpinists around the fells and it was now a dalesman who finished them off.

But there is another long-distance challenge hovering in the northern mist—the Pennine Way. Perhaps now is the time for the Baggers to move over and the Trotters to make their mark. In 1984, Mike Cudahy of the Rucksack Club completed it in a single journey of two days, 21 hours, 54 minutes and 30 seconds. The actual time spent travelling was around 61 hours, the remaining time being spent either sleeping (one hour 37 minutes) or eating and attending to blisters and the like. He had broken the three-day barrier, but to outdo the Bob Graham Round and complete it in 24 hours, which would require an average speed to equal that of a world class marathon, is surely preposterous. Perhaps the time has come for some lateral thinking.

Cudahy calculated the distance at 270 miles but nowadays, with Open Access, you can cut the odd corner or two and with a route of that length you must be able to save quite a few miles. Wainwright put the traditional distance from Tan Hill to Cross Fell at 45 miles, whereas our old friend, the conscientious crow, could cover the same distance in around twenty. No runner would want to follow such a beeline but it should be possible, by choosing the best route, to achieve a saving of twenty miles and, if a number of other kinks were ironed out, keep the total distance to under 250. All this would still be in the spirit of the original route and, in fact, sticks more closely to the concept of a way along the Pennine Chain.

This still seems ridiculous, but the last thought throws up another couple of possibilities. As the Pennine Way is supposed to be a route along the Pennines, neither Kielder Forest nor the hills of Cheviot has any right to feature. The logical place to finish is around Hadrian's Wall and, given the short-cuts already

mentioned, the journey from Edale to, say, Greenhead would be reduced to around 170 miles. (Alternatively, you might consider one of the original plans for the walk—reaching the Tyne Gap via Allendale—and take as direct a line as possible from the Tan Hill Inn to Killhope Law with an earlier finish at Allenheads.)

If this still seems too far, a closer and therefore shorter definition should be sought. You could follow the lead of the Ordnance Survey and start somewhere near the foot of Explorer OL21 (South Pennines)—Marsden would be a suitable point—and follow the Way to the top of Explorer OL31 (North Pennines). By keeping to the high ground after Cross Fell and traversing Melmerby Fell and Hartside before dropping off Byers Pike and finishing at Midgeholme, you might properly claim to have completed the real Pennine Way and also cut the challenge to nearer 150 miles. Nevertheless, to maintain an average speed of more than 6mph for 24 hours is still a big ask. But a hundred years ago, the possibility of completing the Bob Graham Round would have been dismissed out of hand. Yet in half that time the total number of peaks ascended in 24 hours has been nearly doubled.

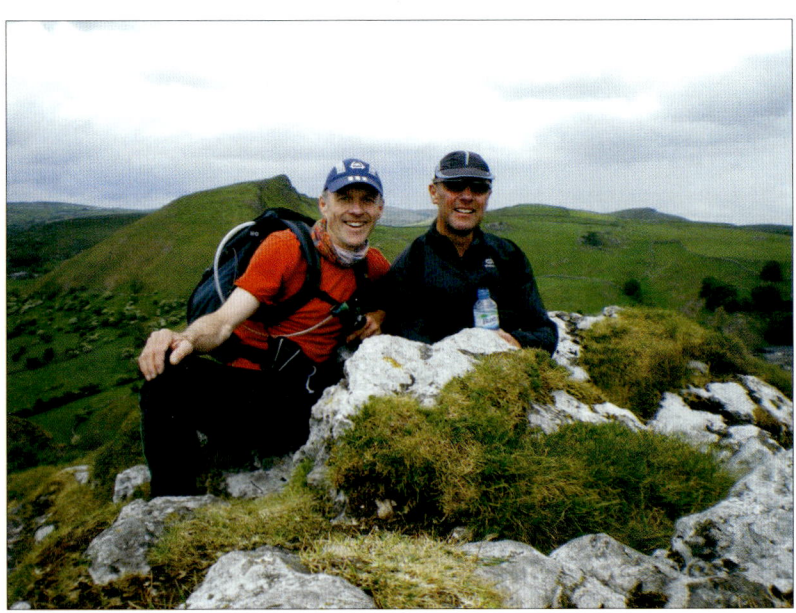

Chris Harle and twin brother Colin on Parkhouse Hill

Postscript
by Chris Harle

During one of our many meetings at the King's Head in Buxton, Graham reminded me of W H Murray's description of a one-day traverse of Rannoch Moor in the summer heatwave of 1949. Although there is an obvious logic to attempting such a challenge walk when the summer months afford extended daylight hours and drier conditions, Murray concludes his chapter contemplating the wonders and enchantment of winter scenery. In fine weather 'a winter traverse of the whole moor would give a man these and other things, and an adventure into the bargain.'

Thus prompted, we recognise that completing a Forty Plus route over two days during the winter is no less a challenge, and perhaps a journey to be savoured. In January 2012 I took advantage of a favourable forecast to finish my reconnaissance of Northumberland's 'Hot Trod'. In my post-Christmas state of unfitness and with only about eight-and-a-half hours of daylight available, I was never going to be able to do the 44-mile walk in a day. So I loaded my sack with camping equipment and provisions and set off from Wooler, wallowing in the crystal clear landscape but not in the mud.

Over two near-perfect days the frost hardened farm tracks and sludge, and knee-deep moorland bog had firmed up enough to allow a direct passage through sections where you would normally have to endure tiresome squelchy detours. St Cuthbert's Way, the Border Ridge and The Cheviot had never looked so good, making up for previous visits when rather dreich conditions were suffered and nothing was seen during a heads-down slog through the mist. On this occasion I raced to the summit trig point of The Cheviot in an attempt to beat the sun dipping behind me in the west. I only just about won and in a photographic frenzy dashed around snapping self-timed poses. I lingered as orange hues tinted my surroundings and the day came to a glorious close.

The temperature and darkness plummeted in tandem as I reluctantly set off to Windy Gyle over five miles away. No map

was needed as a friendly paved way assuredly snaked southwards in the beam of my head-torch. Where the slabs were iced over, a silvery reflection of the night sky gave warning and I confidently bounded over the creaking surface. Thankfully, the summit of Windy Gyle at 2031 feet did not live up to its name. Well-practised moves soon had the tent pitched and me inside luxuriating in the warmth of a down sleeping bag. With my head in England and my feet in Scotland I sipped whiskey-laced coffee, marvelled at the miracle of lightweight tent fabric and contentedly enjoyed the gastronomic delights of pot noodle and chocolate bars.

Later, a call of nature could not be stalled any further and I grumpily dressed to face the chilly night air. I stepped out into an amazing, non-polluted astral light show. Most prominent was the constellation Orion, with its sword pointing directly to my summit campsite. More photographs were taken with numbing fingers clumsily pressing the small buttons on my compact digital camera. No prizes for artwork but a visual reminder nevertheless.

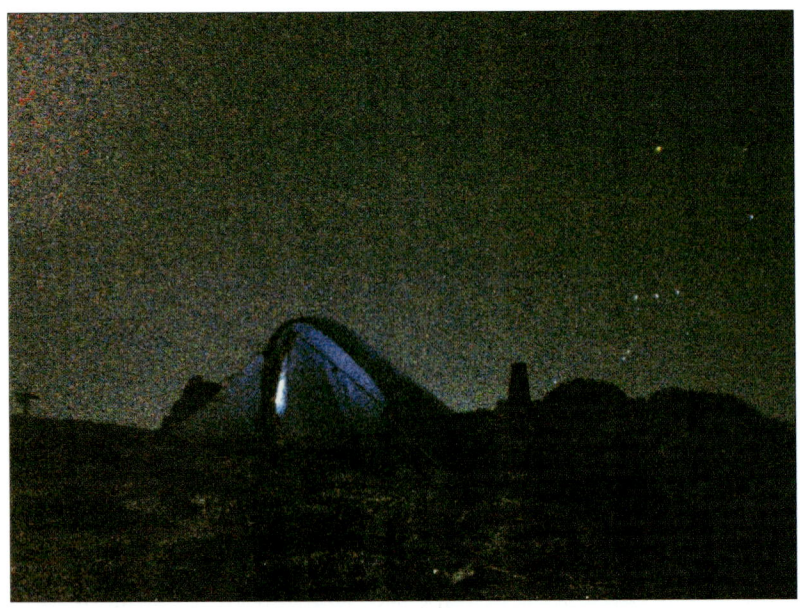

Starlit Windy Gyle campsite

As expected, the morning sunrise did not disappoint. I could not help but gasp 'Wow!' as the eastern horizon was set ablaze by the re-emergent sun. It was a fleeting moment but enough to set me off with a buoyant spring in my step. Delicate frost-encrusted grass and tiny hanging icicles decorated my descent towards the remote farm at Uswayford where chimney smoke hung lazily in the still air. I expected my return to Wooler to be an anticlimax following the previous day's highs. However, the route back offered a constant change of terrain and interest, especially the partly frozen waterfall at Linhope Spout. As my journey neared its end, distant snow patches winked at me in the flickering sunlight while the rising moon chased the shy winter sun horizon-bound. Black icy patches on the tundra-like surface continued to send me into crazed pirouettes and I giggled at my inelegant attempts to stay upright.

I revelled in the remoteness of this area, meeting few people over the two days. At this time of year the *Hot Trod* was more of a *Cold Trod*, but all the better for that.

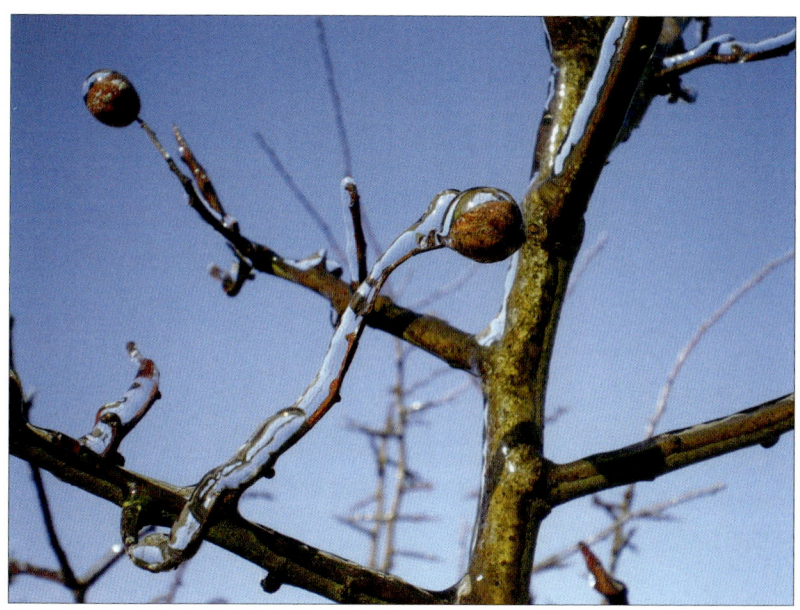

Ice-encrusted branch

Other books by Graham Wilson and Chris Harle

Outdoor titles (originally published by Millrace but now part of Bâton Wicks, an imprint of Vertebrate Publishing)

Chris Harle and Graham Wilson

Mountain Words: British Hill & Crag Literature into the 21st Century, 2009

Graham Wilson

Macc & the Art of Long Distance Walking, 1998 and 2007

Climbing Down, 2002

Macc & Other Islands, 2004

A Measure of Munros, 2005

A Rope of Writers, 2006

Tops of the North, vol I, 2008

Tops of the North, vol II, 2009

Over the Hill, a string of mountain matters, 2011

The Central Buttress of Scafell (ed), a collection of early Fell & Rock Club and YRCC journal articles, 2004

'A Tale of Two Trails' in *A Bit of Grit on Haystacks, A Celebration of Wainwight*, ed Dave Hewitt, 2004

Other titles by Graham Wilson

Mickey Braddock's Works Do and Other Stories, Millrace, 1999

Shakespeare & the Common Man, Millrace, 2001

English Rugby: A Game of Two Halves, Millrace, 2003

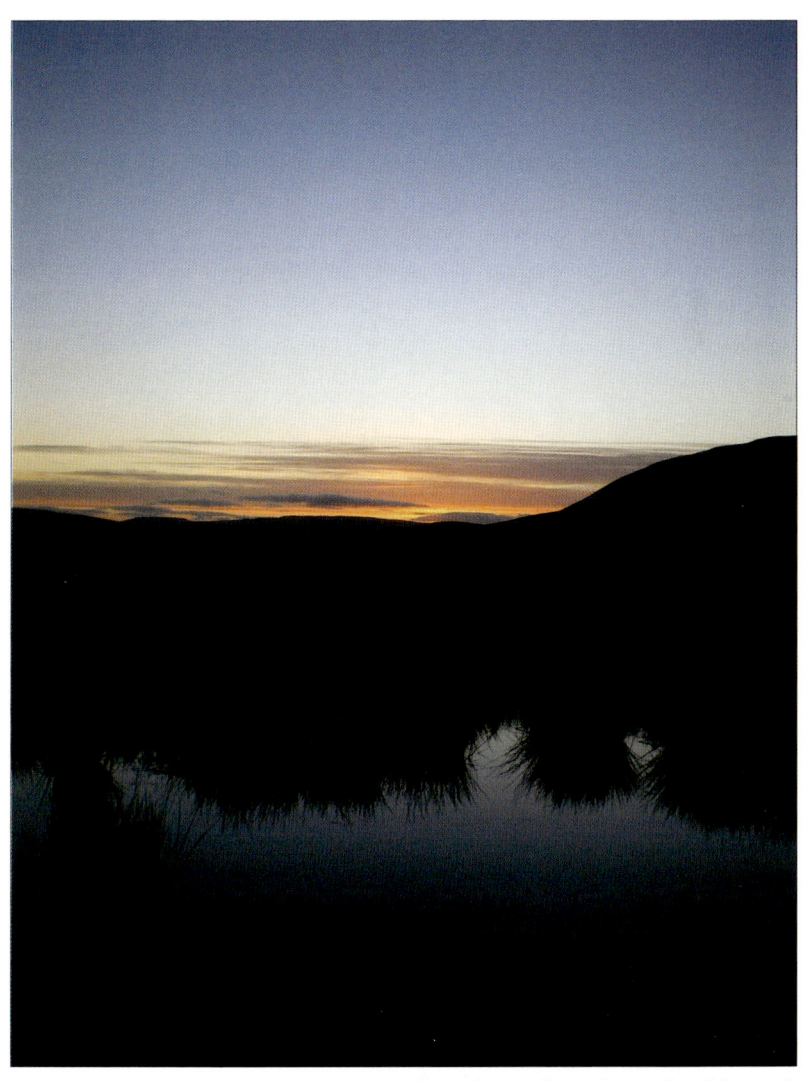

Sunrise from the northern slopes of Ingleborough

Reader's Log

The authors would be interested to hear from readers who have completed all or any of these routes, with particular reference to any changes they may have found: hightorpublications@gmail.com

Route	Date	Time	Weather	Party	Comment
The Lang Stride					
Harrier's Delight					
The Cumbrian Watershed					
A Bridge Far Enough					
The Hot Trod					
The Real Pennine Way?					
Three Peaks & One or Two Others					
The M62 Roundabout					
The Bakewell Pudding